LANDMARK

CW00370063

Gran Canaria

Christopher Turner

ABOUT THE AUTHOR

Christopher Turner is the author of London Step-by-Step, which won the 1985 Guidebook of the Year Award. He recently completed a new guide to Sri Lanka, and his two Indian guides to Goa and Kerala & the South, and Bruges are available from Landmark Publishing.

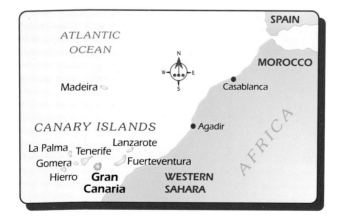

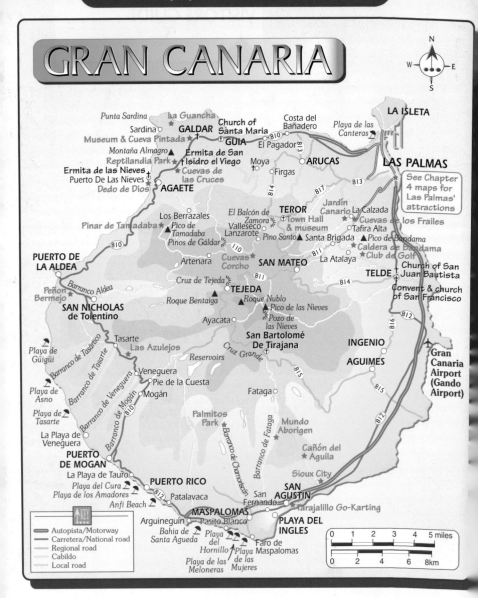

GRAN CANARIA

Punta Sardina
La Guancha
GALDAR ✝
Church of Santa Maria
Costa del Bañadero
Playa de las Canteras ✥
LA ISLETA

Sardina
Museum & Cueva Pintada ★
✝ **GUIA**
810
813
El Pagador
Moya ✝
✝ **ARUCAS**
Playa de las Canteras ✥
LAS PALMAS

Montaña Almagro ▲
Ermita de San ★ **Isidro el Viego**
Reptilandia Park ★
✥ **Cuevas de las Cruces**
Firgas ○

Ermita de las Nieves ✝
Puerto De Las Nieves ✝
Dedo de Dios ·
AGAETE
814
817
813
See Chapter 4 maps for Las Palmas' attractions

Los Berrazales ○
El Balcón de Zamora ○
TEROR
Jardin Canario ✥
La Calzada
★ **Cuevas de los Frailes**

Pinar de Tamadaba ★
Pico de Tamadaba ▲
Valleseco ○
Lanzarote ○
✝ Town Hall & museum
Tafira Alta ○

Pinos de Gáldar ★
Pino Santo ○ ▲
Santa Brigada ▲
▲ Pico de Bandama

PUERTO DE LA ALDEA
810
Artenara ○
Cuevas Corcho ✥
110
SAN MATEO
811
La Atalaya ○
Caldera de Bandama ○
★ Club de Golf

Peñon Bermejo
Barranco Aldea
Cruz de Tejeda ✥
Roque Bentaiga ▲
▲ **TEJEDA**
Roque Nublo ▲
Pico de las Nieves ▲
814
TELDE ✝ Church of San Juan Bautista

SAN NICHOLAS de Tolentino
Ayacata ○
Pozo de las Nieves ☆
Convent & church of San Francisco

Tasarte ○
Las Azulejos ○
Cruz Grande
San Bartolomé De Tirajana
INGENIO
816
812

Playa de Güigüi
Barranco de Tasarte
Reservoirs
AGUIMES
815
Gran Canaria Airport (Gando Airport)

Playa de Asno
Barranco de Veneguera
Veneguera ○
Pie de la Cuesta ○
Fataga ○
815

Playa de Tasarte
Barranco de Mogán
Mogán ○
Palmitos Park ★
Mundo Aborigen ★
812

La Playa de Veneguera ○
810
Barranco de Chamoriscal
Cañón del Aguila ★

PUERTO DE MOGAN
Barranco de Fataga
Sioux City ★

La Playa de Tauro ○
PUERTO RICO
Patalavaca ○
San Fernando ○
SAN AGUSTIN
Tarajalillo Go-Karting

Playa del Cura ☆
Playa de los Amadores ☆
812
SAN AGUSTIN

Anfi Beach ○
MASPALOMAS
Pasito Blanco ○
PLAYA DEL INGLES

Arguineguin ○
Bahia de Santa Agueda
Playa del Hornillo
Faro de Maspalomas
Playa de las Mujeres

Playa de las Meloneras

0   1   2   3   4   5 miles
0   2   4   6   8km

KEY
— Autopista/Motorway
— Carretera/National road
— Regional road
— Cabildo
— Local road

Publishers note:

• The capital of Gran Canaria is Las Palmas de Gran Canaria, throughout this book it is refered to as Las Palmas.

• In this guide book we refer to the airport as 'Gando Airport', the airport has officially changed it's name to 'Gran Canaria Airport'.

• The Galerias Preciados department store has been taken over by El Corte Inglés.

Gran Canaria

CONTENTS

TOP TIPS

To assist tourists with limited time available, especially if making their first visit to Gran Canaria, locations of major interest have been selected. Some will have particular appeal for children and are indicated accordingly.

MASPALOMAS SAND DUNES (page 31)

Stretching from Maspalomas lighthouse to Playa del Inglés, these golden dunes evoke the nearby Sahara Desert and have provided backgrounds for many fashion photographers.

PUERTO DE MOGÁN (page 38)

This man-made Venetian-style yacht marina is the most visually pleasing of all the tourist developments in the Canaries.

PALMITOS PARK (page 47)

Exotic birds, many of them flying freely, combined with sub-tropical plants and rare butterflies provide the island's most popular tourist attraction.

THE CENTRAL MOUNTAINS (page 51)

The centrepiece of the volcanic mountain range in the middle of the island is Roque Nublo, the world's loftiest slab of baltic rock.

SIOUX CITY (page 48)

This 'American Wild West' attraction occupies a set originally built for a film. Obviously, its primary appeal is to youngsters and western film enthusiasts.

VEGUETA, LAS PALMAS (page 64)

Las Palmas was founded in its Vegueta Quarter, where ancient buildings include the picturesque Columbus Museum, where the discoverer of America is believed to have lodged prior to his voyage, and the Cathedral de Santa Ana. Both are 15th century foundations.

LAS CANTERAS BEACH, LAS PALMAS (page 71)

Voted among the top ten beaches of the world, not only is Las Canteras scenic, but its golden sands are protected by a narrow reef of rock, and are ultra safe for children.

AVENIDA JOSÉ MESA Y LÓPEZ, LAS PALMAS (page 76)

Located in the Alcaravaneras Quarter, this thoroughfare incorporates branches of Spain's most prestigious stores, including El Corte Inglés and Galerías Preciados.

'PARADISE' ROUTE (page 92)

From the Jardín Canario, via San Mateo, the 811 road to the mountains passes through some of the most idyllic, verdant scenery in the Canaries – spiky palm trees jostle for position with the feathery eucalyptus.

Although the Mediterranean resorts are often promoted as winter-sun holiday destinations, the winter rainfall of most usually exceeds considerably that of the south coast of England. But by flying due south for less than one hour longer, often at no greater cost, the chill north winds will at last have petered out, and a warm sun will be shining almost without interruption. The Canary Islands, 'The Fortunate Isles', have been reached.

However, the Canaries are far from being just a winter holiday destination. In mid-summer, when their temperatures are only moderately higher, the climate is, once again, nigh perfect: the scorching heat of the Mediterranean will rarely be approached.

Those who select Gran Canaria from the other islands in the group as their holiday destination are chiefly attracted by its golden sand beaches (which include the famous Sahara-style sand dunes of Maspalomas), its dramatic mountains, the idyllic pastoral scenery of the island's north, and the fascinating, cosmopolitan city of Las Palmas.

Apart from the old quarter of Las Palmas, the Maspalomas lighthouse, and an occasional defensive tower, there are no vintage buildings of architectural interest to be found along the entire coastline of Gran Canaria: the fishing villages were always poor, and their inhabitants quite unable to afford the splendid balconies and decorated churches that are a feature of the more prosperous inland towns, such as Teror, Telde and Arucas. A similar situation occurs in all the other islands of the archipelago, and

those seeking quaint fishing villages overlooking unspoilt beaches of golden sand will be disappointed. Having said this, however, the occasional excursion to a coastal *tapas* bar, where the atmosphere is truly Spanish, provides a refreshing change from the unreality of the tourist resorts (and so do the prices).

Some visitors will spend most of their holiday relaxing on a sandy beach, perhaps only leaving it during the day to purchase duty-free drinks and tobacco in Gran Canaria's irresistible shops. Others will prefer to make excursions to other parts of this beautiful island. *Landmark Visitor's Guide: Gran Canaria* provides invaluable assistance to both categories. Each resort is explored in depth: not all of them are ideal for everybody, although very few holidaymakers will have difficulty in choosing a location on the island that suits them perfectly.

Although many itineraries are described in great detail, with all the roads identified, not everyone will have a car at all times, therefore appropriate bus information is also provided. Although the island's two bus companies have merged, it is not planned to change the bus numbers.

The aim of this book is to ensure that you make the utmost of your Gran Canaria holiday, whenever you go, wherever you stay and whatever your interests. It will prove to be a tremendous time and money saver.

GEOGRAPHY

Gran Canaria is one of seven islands that, accompanied by six tiny islets, make up the Canary Islands (Islas Canarias), renowned since ancient times for their benign all-year round climate. Probably to overcome this unlucky number of 13, another island has been 'sighted' on the horizon from time to time, and even named – San Borondon. Volcanic in origin, the islands form an archipelago lying just off Morocco's Atlantic coastline, approximately 515km (320 miles) north of the Tropic of Cancer. From west to east, they comprise: El Hierro, La Palma, La Gomera, Tenerife, Gran Canaria, Lanzarote and Fuerteventura.

Gran Canaria, Fuerteventura and Lanzarote together form a province of Spain, administered from Las Palmas, which is the eighth largest city in the country.

Venture inland

Gran Canaria, an almost circular island, the third largest in the group, covers an area of 1,532 sq km (591 sq miles). Apart from a short interruption at the western extremity, a main road follows its entire coastline, which enthusiastic motorists can therefore see in just one day. Expeditions to the interior, however, take much longer: roads zig-zag, climb and descend, and what appears from the map to involve a reasonably short journey can take up much of the day. Nevertheless, those who forego visiting the north and centre of Gran Canaria will be missing the very essence of the island: craggy mountain peaks towering over slender eucalyptus trees, exuberant palms, prickly cacti and lush orchards, and everywhere, and at all seasons, bougainvillaea, with its brilliant red, purple, white and orange blossom enlivening the white walls of pastoral cottages.

Roque Nublo

Puerto de Mogán has the most scenic backdrop of the southern resorts

FLORA

Approximately 2,000 species of plants have been identified on Gran Canaria, some of them unique to the archipelago. Canary Pines and Canary Palms are varieties found nowhere else, but the most spectacular 'tree' is undoubtedly a strange survivor from the earth's Tertiary Period, the dragon tree (*dracaneo draco*), examples of which have lived for several thousand years.

Apart from the ubiquitous bougainvillaea, most flowers will be familiar to north European holidaymakers, although some of them only as pot plants. Particularly impressive is the poinsettia, bushes of which grow wild along the roadsides to a great height – some pot plant! A flower that

Above: Fan palm
Left: Hibiscus

cannot be grown in Europe, but which has come to represent the Canaries' flora, is the *strelitzia*, better known as the Bird of Paradise flower. Many tourists return home clutching bunches of this yellow and purple flower, which they have bought at the last moment: the waxy blooms have an unusually long life. As may be expected, cacti thrive in the dry south.

None of the Canary crops is indigenous to the islands, each being a post-colonisation introduction. The Roman historian Pliny referred to date palms and olives, but many centuries were to pass before sugar cane, vines, mangoes, papayas, potatoes, yams, avocados, tomatoes and bananas were introduced. Tomatoes are now by far the most important export crop, followed by cucumbers, aubergines and onions. The price of locally-grown bananas, which are exceptionally tasty, is now undercut by third-world countries, thereby making them uneconomic to grow commercially. Almonds, roses and carnations remain profitable exports, as do the delicious, tiny Canary potatoes, although production is limited, most of it going to Spain. Some wine is still produced, but only sufficient for local consumption. Game birds are plentiful and, during the season, August-December, they may be found on the menus of the more expensive restaurants.

FAUNA

The fauna of Gran Canaria is less spectacular than its flora, even the plentiful rabbits and large lizards rarely appearing for tourists. Birds of prey are only usually spied in the mountains; they may include white eagles, buzzards and hawks, all of which hunt smaller birds. Two hundred birds have been identified but, bird enthusiasts will seek in vain for bright-yellow canaries (named from the islands rather than the other way round) flying free, as the natural colouring of this bird is primarily brown, with just a few yellow streaks. Only in captivity do all its feathers turn yellow, and only the male bird sings.

The waters around the Canaries are well stocked with fish, but species are rather limited. Most numerous are tuna, mackerel, sardines and swordfish, plus several local varieties: including cherne and viejas. Shellfish is almost non-existent, only small shrimps, winkles and limpets finding these coasts to their liking.

CLIMATE

The Canary Islands' moderate temperatures are their greatest attraction; almost never, at least at lower levels, will the visitor feel cold; and rarely will temperatures exceed 29°C (85°F). Rainfall is light, almost negligible in the south, most of it usually occurring between mid-November and mid-March. Sunshine, however, is rather less predictable; September, October and March being generally, but not always, the sunniest months. Annoyingly, in the south, midwinter, when most visit the island, is often the cloudiest period. To emphasise that the climate of Gran Canaria is far from predictable, the November to mid-March period in 1994/5 was completely dry.

Although British and Spanish tourists favour the summer months, most other foreigners visit between November and February, to escape the cold and dark of the northern winters. Almost all tourists now stay on the south coast of the island, where the sun shines more reliably than further north. However, beaches immediately south of the airport are all of dark volcanic sand and favoured primarily by local families that want to avoid the tourists, sharing them only with the fishermen.

Due to its low rainfall, the countryside immediately behind the south coast is predominantly arid, giving no hint of the verdant, paradisical scenery further north.

There are dramatic differences in the sunshine figures for Puerto Rico and Las Palmas, the former resort, together with Puerto de Mogán, being the sunniest on the island. Canarios claim that the location of Aeropuerto de Gando, Gran Canaria's international airport, frequently marks the island's climatic division – usually cloudy to the north of it, sunny to the south. Climate statistics for Gran Canaria are measured at the airport, and do not accurately represent the situation at either Las Palmas or the southern resorts. When, on occasions, the wind blows from the south-west rather than the usual north-east, everything can change, with the north having clearer weather. A south-east sirocco wind from the Sahara blows usually twice a year, bearing with it desert sand. This is most unpleasant, the sky becomes yellow and the sun all but disappears; those with weak chests are advised to stay indoors to avoid the choking air. Fortunately, the sirocco rarely blows for more than three days.

Las Palmas lies in a bowl, surrounded by mountains, and air pollution is a great problem during the summer, when a heavy smog known as *panza de burro* (donkey's stomach) hangs over the city, blotting out the sun. July and August are definitely the worst months for a Las Palmas holiday.

At any time of the year, visitors are advised to take warm clothing with them when visiting the high mountains, which reach a height of 1,949m (6,393ft) at the summit of Pico de las Nieves, and are frequently cloudy. Even on the coast during the winter months a jacket or sweater may well be needed from early evening until mid morning, particularly if a wind is blowing.

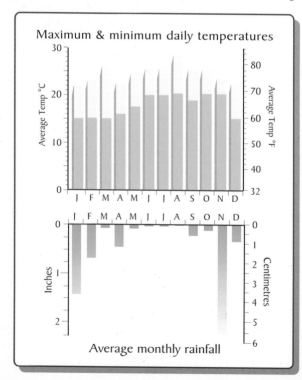

Maximum & minimum daily temperatures

Average monthly rainfall

HISTORY

Because the Canary Islands, although located more than 1,000km (600 miles) from the Iberian peninsula, have long been an integral part of Spain, their history since the late fifteenth century incorporates that of the entire country. However, in this section events only specific to Gran Canaria are outlined.

A surprise to many is that the Canary Islands, adjacent to the African coast, are classed officially as part of Europe, indeed they are within the European Union (but not for Customs purposes).

Myths & early history

It is believed that the Canary Islands arose from the sea bed as part of volcanic activity 140 million years ago. The first certain reference to the archipelago was by Pliny the Elder (AD23-79), who recorded an expedition to it by King Juba of Mauretania in AD30. Puzzlingly, he refers to the ruins of great buildings, and a complete lack of inhabitants apart from large dogs (*canis* in Latin, and the source of the Canaries' name), two of which were captured. It was also Pliny who first dubbed the group 'The Fortunate Isles'.

Plaza de Santa Ana, in Vegueta

The Guanches

In spite of Pliny's description of uninhabited islands – possibly the natives were in hiding – Arab merchants appear to have traded with Gran Canaria around 1000AD. The people that they would have traded with are known as Guanches, a Canary word derived from *guan* (men) and *achinech* (white mountain), an obvious reference to Tenerife's snow-clad Mount Teide. Only the natives of Tenerife were originally called Guanches, but eventually the name was applied to all the aboriginal islanders. Who were these people, and where did they come from? Many of them are known to have had fair hair and pale eyes, leading anthropologists to suggest a Scandinavian origin. However, it has been pointed out that some Berbers from the North-African mountains possess similar features, and their close proximity to the islands makes them more likely candidates.

The Guanches have long been extinct, although inter-breeding with their Spanish conquerors obviously occurred. What is known is that the Guanches lived a Neolithic, stone-age existence, which had advanced little over the centuries. They could not write, nor were they navigators, little contact being made between the inhabitants of the various islands in spite of the short distances that separated them. The Guanches lived primarily in caves, some of which still retain evidence of their occupancy, kept goats and pigs, and operated a primitive form of agriculture dependant on maize for grinding into a flour that is still known as *gofio*.

Rediscovery

Strangely, the existence of the Canaries seems to have been forgotten, at least by Europeans, until the Genoese, Lancellotto Mallocello, 'rediscovered' them early in the fourteenth century. He eventually charted a map of the islands, immodestly naming one of them Lanzarote, after himself. Merchants from Spain, Portugal and Italy now began to trade with the Guanches and, from the information they provided, Angelino Dulcert, a Majorcan cartographer, prepared the first accurate map of the archipelago in 1339.

Trading now continued apace and in 1342 the island's first bishopric was created by Pope Clement VI, at Telde, now Gran Canaria's second most important town. Friars soon arrived from Majorca, then part of the powerful state of Catalonia, bent on converting the natives to Christianity. No acts of aggression, however, were perpetrated against the inhabitants until, in 1393, Alvaro Becerra from Seville, carried out sorties to capture Guanches for enslavement in Spain. During one of these, he fearfully witnessed a spectacular eruption of Mount Teide, and dubbed Tenerife 'Hell Island'.

Spanish colonisation

Enríquez III of Castile gave the order for Spanish colonisation of the Canary Islands to begin in 1402, commissioning Jean de Bethencourt, a Norman baron, to take, in the name of Christianity, the least populated islands: Lanzarote, Fuerteventura, La Gomera and El Hierro. In spite of their primitive weapons, the Guanches, aided by the mountainous terrain, offered stiff opposition, and it was not until 1496 that the largest island, Tenerife, was finally taken by the Spanish. At one time, the Portuguese briefly occupied some of the islands, but the Treaty of Alcaçovas, in 1480, ended their ambitions in the islands.

Spaniards invaded Gran Canaria in 1478, Juan Rejón immediately setting up an encampment at Las Palmas. Here again, the Guanches proved strong opponents, and the whole island did not fall until 1483, when Pedro de Vera wiped out the last pockets of resistance. He had been aided by Semidan, a renegade Guanche leader, who was eventually baptised and renamed Fernando.

In a remarkably short space of time, the Guanches completely disappeared as an identifiable race. Many of them had been killed in battle, and some taken into slavery, but the survivors had no resistance against European diseases, which decimated them. Some interbred with their conquerors, and there may still be seen blonde-haired Canarios that betray Guanche ancestry. The initial Spanish encampment at Las Palmas quickly spread eastward across the Guiniguada ravine, which came to serve as a dividing line between the houses of the well-to-do and those of the working classes. El Real de las Palmas was founded on 23 June 1478 and incorporated in the crown of Castile: it was the first city in the Canaries.

An early visitor was Christopher Columbus, who docked at Las Palmas for repairs to be made to his vessels on route to discover America in 1492.

Poverty to prosperity

For long, most Canarios belonged to poverty-struck agricultural and fishing communities, only the importance of Santa Cruz de Tenerife and Las Palmas as convenient calling stages for transatlantic merchant ships creating any appreciable income. Peninsular Spain had declined rapidly as a major power since the late sixteenth century, and no investment from the mainland could be expected: the Canaries went into virtual isolation.

Following Napoleon's defeat at Waterloo, and Spain's demise as a combatant nation, many British emigrated to Las Palmas, and soon began to influence the commercial development of the islands. By the mid-nineteenth century, prosperity had brought an end to the isolation of Las Palmas: public buildings were erected, its enclosing wall demolished and, in 1852, the Canary Islands, as a group, were designated a free port by royal decree.

Las Canteras Beach at Christmas

Rapid nineteenth-century development

Fernando León y Castillo, from Telde, Gran Canaria's second largest city, was appointed Spain's Foreign Minister, and became instrumental in the realisation of the new port of Las Palmas, known as Puerto de la Luz (Port of Light). The project, engineered by his brother, was an immediate success, and trade quickly outstripped that of its Tenerife rival, Santa Cruz. By the turn of the century, Las Palmas had been adopted by the British navy as its Atlantic base.

Around this time, two important crops were introduced to the Canaries: tomatoes and bananas. The latter was the inspiration of the Englishman, Alfred L Jones, and his name, under its Spanish adaptation Alfredo, has been given to one of the major streets leading to Las Canteras beach. British companies soon gained a virtual monopoly in the export of both tomatoes and bananas from the Canaries.

The twentieth century

World War I, throughout which Spain remained neutral, saw a further upsurge in émigrés from Europe, many of them wealthy refugees, and the already cosmopolitan nature of Las Palmas was consolidated.

It was from Gran Canaria that General Franco, then Captain General of the island's military and civil affairs, unleashed the Spanish Civil War in 1936, but the islands suffered little, compared with peninsular Spain, from the four years of turmoil that followed.

During World War II, Hitler pressurised Franco to permit the German navy to operate a base at Las

The harbour at Puerto de Mogán

Palmas in exchange for the promise of eventually presenting him with Gibraltar, but Spain insisted on remaining neutral. Not long after the war ended, Las Palmas, with its constantly warm climate and outstanding beach, evolved into an international tourist resort, and was followed, in the early 1960s, by the development of tourist resorts on the island's sunny south coast. Not everyone prospered, however, and discontent led to 8,000 leaving the Canaries illegally, many of them settling in South America, Venezuela in particular. In the early 1950s, Franco legalised emigration, and a further 150,000 departed from the islands. Franco died in 1975, having appointed Juan Carlos, the present king, as his successor.

Although Spain joined the EEC in 1986, and Gran Canaria, as part of its province of Las Palmas, is therefore a member, it has been permitted to remain outside the EU Customs Union, and designated a free trade zone. As in the rest of Spain, the world recession of the 1990s hit the Canary Islands particularly hard and, in 1995, unemployment in Las Palmas reached approximately 30 per cent. Partly due to this, crimes such as pickpocketing, mugging and burglary rocketed, with tourists being prime targets. Care should still be taken, and quiet parts of Las Palmas avoided at night. Tourism, however, is steadily increasing, and the reborn fashionability of ocean-liner cruising is a welcome supplement to the income of Puerto de la Luz, the international port of Las Palmas.

FOOD & DRINK

Food lovers are urged, if possible, to book their Gran Canaria hotel on a bed and breakfast basis, otherwise they risk being condemned to tasteless, repetitive 'international' meals, which soon begin to pall. Remember that the hotelier is working on a very tight budget, and also that he wishes to avoid complaints by unsophisticated guests about unfamiliar, 'funny-tasting' dishes. Rarely will he offer anything Spanish, apart, perhaps, from an occasional watery *paella*, and *gazpacho*; local specialities will most certainly not be provided.

Families and younger visitors sometimes opt to interrupt the boredom of hotel meals with the occasional foray to a fast-food outlet, pizzas, pastas, burgers, frankfurters, spit-roasted chickens, and chips (but not fish and chips) being readily available at reasonable prices in all the resorts virtually 24 hours a day. A grade up are restaurants, most of which, like the hotels, serve international dishes, but of a much higher quality; the meat, in particular, is usually excellent, most of the beef and lamb coming from South America.

Ethnic restaurants exist in the resorts but few offer authentic dishes. The most commonly served Canary speciality is *papas arrugadas*, 'wrinkled' potatoes, cooked in salted water and served in their jackets with

Tapas bars

Unfortunately, although Gran Canaria is part of Spain, *tapas* bars are far less numerous, particularly at the southern resorts, than in the peninsula, and the variety and quality of their dishes are much lower. The vast majority of holidaymakers who stay in the south will find it necessary to make for either Arguineguín, a resort between Puerto Rico and Maspalomas, or San Fernando, a 'Spanish' enclave, which is virtually a suburb of Playa del Inglés, in order to track down a genuine *tapas* bar. As may be expected, Las Palmas and the inland towns are much better provided. Remember that a *tapas* is a very small, saucer-size portion, while a *ración* is much larger; some dishes are available only in *ración* sizes.

Throughout peninsular Spain, the emphasis in a *tapas* bar is on shellfish, but this is virtually non-existent in the waters of the Canary Islands. Imported *gambas* (large prawns) will be deep-frozen and lack the flavour of the fresh version. For this reason, Canarios rarely eat them.

piquant mojo sauce. Others are explained in the Food Vocabulary in the FactFile.

Tap water is drinkable in Gran Canaria, but tastes rather unpleasant. Most will prefer to purchase large bottles of mineral water – gas or non-gas – which is much more palatable, particularly when refrigerated. The local, and most popular brand, is Firgas.

To summarise, Gran Canaria is hardly a gourmet's paradise, but those who make the effort to seek out the limited number of local specialities, which have evolved through Guanche traditions, Spanish tastes and Latin-American influences, are in for a pleasurable, as well as an interesting experience.

CHOOSING A RESORT

Until the early 1960s, visitors to Gran Canaria had little option but to stay in Las Palmas, with its wide range of hotels. Since then, the south coast, due to much higher sunshine, has gradually become the major tourist destination. It is split into a south-east facing section, dubbed the Costa Canaria, which is entirely built-up and favoured by the Germans, and a south-west facing section, more extensive but less developed, and preferred by the British. Due to the configuration of the mountains and the prevailing north-east wind, less cloud cover can generally be expected the further west the resort is located.

Las Palmas is still preferred by those willing to trade less guaranteed sunshine for a genuine Spanish atmosphere, much lower prices and the superb Las Canteras beach, rated among the most beautiful in the world. Some UK tour operators, once again include this great city in their programme.

In spite of the fact that Gran Canaria's south coast has been developed over a relatively short period, the main resorts possess individual characteristics that vary greatly, and these should be considered before a resort is selected. The entire stretch is linked by buses, but there are no night services along the west-facing coast, and taxis in the Canary Islands are not cheap. The resorts are, of course, dealt with in detail in this book, but the summary on pages 20-21, from east to west, will help first-time visitors to the island make a quick appraisal of each of them, and judge how they meet their own requirements.

Only the largest hotels boast swimming pools that are heated in winter – but to maximum 25°C!

The main south coast holiday

San Agustín

🙂 **Advantages:** small in size, with most accommodation near the beach, relatively select and quiet, attractive promenades.

🙁 **Disadvantages:** can be cloudy, inconvenient for a varied night life and restaurants, steep approach to some accommodation.

Playa del Inglés

🙂 **Advantages:** extensive night life, good selection of restaurants, wide range of accommodation, regular bus services, many shopping/entertainment centres.

🙁 **Disadvantages:** architecturally characterless, lacks an identifiable centre, few trees and no parks, some accommodation is a long walk from the beach, steep access to the beach, excessive time-share and other touting, generally windy afternoons.

Maspalomas

Punta de Maspalomas divides the east and west-facing stretches of the south coast.

🙂 **Advantages:** dramatic sand dunes, luxury hotels, tranquil lagoon.

🙁 **Disadvantages:** isolated situation, strong afternoon winds.

The recently created beach of Playa de las Amadores just north of Puerto Rico

Pasito Blanco

Advantages: yacht marina, secluded beach, calm sea for divers, good camping site.

Disadvantages: isolated situation, limited shopping, restaurant and entertainment facilities, few hotels.

Arguineguín

Advantages: Canary atmosphere (rare on the south coast) of an established fishing port, good fish restaurants and *tapas* bars, low prices, the La Canaria Hotel is probably the most luxurious on the coast.

Disadvantages: unattractive beach, no night life.

Patalavaca

Advantages: pleasant beachfront promenade, well-kept beach, proximity to the white, coral sand beach of the Anfi time-share development.

Disadvantages: consists entirely of beachfront apartments, limited access to the beach from the road, no nightlife.

Puerto Rico

Advantages: safe golden sand beach, protection from most winds by encompassing hills, verdant parks, game-fishing opportunities, attractive public swimming pool complex heated sufficiently for comfort in winter – unlike the hotel pools!

Disadvantages: long, steep approach to most apartments, little nightlife, run down shopping centre, isolation, almost all accommodation is self-catering, little unreserved accommodation available – particularly in winter. Puerto Rico is dominated in summer by British holidaymakers – to some this is an advantage, to others it is not.

Puerto de Mogán

Advantages: undoubtedly the most architecturally attractive (some say the *only* attractive) development on the coast, vibrant marina, a profusion of flowers, the original port with Canary ambience still survives, highest sunshine record on the coast, boat excursions, outstanding restaurant food.

Disadvantages: somewhat isolated, a neglected grey sand beach, much new construction work, no nightlife, higher prices.

The South-East Coast Resorts

SAN AGUSTÍN

As the first of the Costa Canaria resorts is approached, the delightful **Bahía Feliz** opens up, where conditions are ideal for windsurfing, and championship contests are held. Within this bay, **Playa de Tarajalillo** is an extensive beach, but much of it is gravelly and interspersed with rocks. **Playa del Aguila**, a mixed stone and sand beach is named after the Cañon del Aguila, another of the many dry ravines that are an important feature of this southern coast.

Playa de Morro Besudo, almost 200m (218yd) long, is the most easterly of San Agustín's beaches, but it has a bad reputation as there have been several drownings.

Lying back from the west end of this beach is the Centro Commercial Morro Besudo, one of two shopping centres in the town; the bus station (29 to Maspalomas and Sioux City and 45 to Palmitos Park) is located in front of it.

Playa de San Agustín, renowned for its crystal clear waters and safe swimming, is the next beach reached, and it was behind this that the town developed. All amenities that might be expected are on offer, including surfboard and pedalo rental. The laying out of the 812 Carretera del Sur road to Las Palmas put a temporary halt to development, but it soon recontinued on the north side of the sunken highway. However, the terrain rises fairly steeply, a fact that should be borne in mind by those booking accommodation in this part of San Agustín. Only a narrow strip of land lies between the *carretera* and

the beach until Playa del Inglés is reached.

Casino Palace Nightclub

Between the beach and the highway lies the four star **Meliá Tamarindos Hotel**, incorporating the Casino Palace Nightclub; its floorshow is regarded as the island's finest. At the casino (jacket and tie obligatory for men) the usual gambling tables will be found, including roulette, blackjack and *chemin de fer*. Passports must be presented on arrival.

A large roundabout bridges the *carretera* immediately north of the casino, providing convenient access to San Agustín's market (*mercado*) and much of the town's accommodation. The next bridge across the highway in the direction of Playa del Inglés leads back to the coast and San Agustín's multi-storey shopping centre.

One of the most attractive aspects of San Agustín is its beautifully maintained seafront promenade, which runs with very few breaks all the way to the sand dunes of Maspalomas. Much of the walk is verdant, as seafront buildings have been restricted to single storey level, i.e. bungalows, and their cacti and flower-bedecked walls and gardens are a delight.

PLAYA DEL INGLÉS

A wedge-shaped town, all of which lies to the south of the *carretera*,

SHOPPING CENTRES IN PLAYA DEL INGLÉS

Although the Canary Islands are duty free and taxes are low, little of this saving is now passed on to the purchaser, and bargains are rare. In 1999 all shops were forced to remove duty free signs.

The **Yumbo Centrum**, the largest shopping complex in Playa del Inglés, is the town's most obvious landmark. The west side of the centre lies slightly back from Avenida de Tirajana, although the approach paths from it are poorly indicated and easily missed. Buses stop by the south entrance. The multi-storey complex is approximately rectangular, its north and south sides being almost twice the length of the other two.

Like most of the coastal shopping centres, the Yumbo Centrum combines supermarkets, boutiques and electronic/camera/watch shops, with bars and restaurants, most of which, but not all, are fast food establishments. A most helpful Tourist Office is located beside the south entance.

Other shopping centres, although smaller, are similar in content and atmosphere. To the south of Yumbo Centrum lies **Cita**, to the south-east **Sandia** and to the east, facing each other, **Kasbah** and **Metro**. Metro is also known as Plaza de Maspalomas, after its central square, which is confusing to most tourists as the centre is nowhere near Faro de Maspalomas. At the eastern end of Playa del Inglés, just south of the *carretera*, are two more shopping centres, which adjoin: **El Viril** and **El Aguila**.

Playa del Inglés, it must be admitted, is not to everyone's taste. Basically, it should be regarded as a convenient dormitory that does not really come to life until sundown, when the bars, restaurants and shopping centres get into their swing – and stay swinging until the small hours. Although Playa del Inglés, due to its haphazard development, lacks memorable architecture, its excellent bus services, not only link all the shopping centres, but also provide easy access to the adjacent beaches and other parts of the island. There is also a varied nightlife, excellent restaurants to suit all tastes and pockets and, of course, there is the superb all-year-round climate, the swimming pools, and the great sweep of golden sand, which merges with the picturesque dunes of Maspalomas.

Playa del Inglés has a high ratio of hotels to self-catering units, but surprisingly only two of them, both four-star, directly overlook the beach: the Dunamar and the Riu Palace, the first of which has the

Yumbo Centrum

unique advantage of a lift that transports guests the six floors between beach and street levels, thus avoiding the rather arduous climb that others (without cars) must make. Just in front of the Dunamar stretches the **Paseo Maritimo**, a half-mile stretch of bars and restaurants directly fronting the sea. Note that its occasional supermarkets are somewhat expensive.

The Riu Palace Hotel juts out at the most southerly tip of Playa del Inglés, and is the most convenient point from which to reach the sand dunes of Maspalomas, which it overlooks. A public pathway leads to them between the two blocks of the hotel, and there is a handy bus stop nearby. On the north side of the hotel, the main thoroughfare, Avenida de Tirajana, stretches northward for almost two miles in a reasonably straight line, even crossing the *carretera* into the 'Spanish' suburb of San Fernando. Do not attempt to walk this rather uninteresting and tiring avenue from end to end in one go; buses traverse most of its length (although all except the 72 turn off westward at Plaza Telde, the avenue's last roundabout before the *carretera* is reached).

The centrally-located **Yumbo Centrum**, the largest shopping centre in Playa del Inglés, provides the town's most obvious landmark. At its south-east corner, the Tourist Information Centre's, helpful staff can provide information about accommodation, public transport, car hire, restaurants, coach tours and special events throughout the island.

After the shops close at around 9pm, the Yumbo Centrum's restaurants take over and the bars open, many of the latter being sparsely

(cont'd on page 29)

Playa del Inglés origin and popularity

The beach was formerly known as El Inglés (the Englishman) due, it is said, to an eccentric Englishman who, some years ago, camped on it for many months in splendid isolation. A more prosaic explanation for the name is that English sailors landed there during the Napoleonic wars. It is certain, however, that 'Inglés' does not refer to English tourists, who are greatly outnumbered, particularly in the more expensive high season (winter), by Germans. In the

summer, which is the cheaper, low season, the British, plus Spaniards escaping from their blisteringly hot mainland peninsula, are more numerous. It seems likely that the difference in wealth between the British and the Germans, rather than taste, is the main reason for this. Scandinavians, bent on escaping their dark, freezing winters, naturally prefer to visit the Canaries from December to May, and are spread fairly evenly among the south coast resorts.

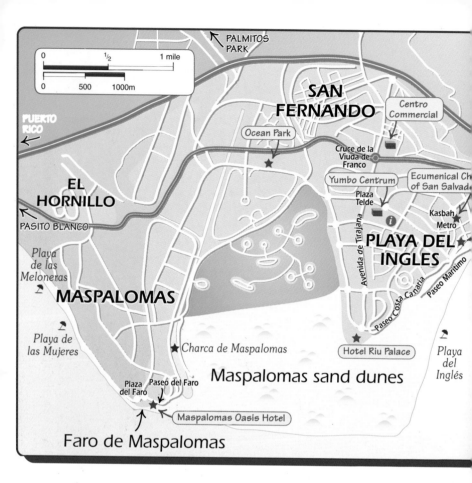

Where to stay in Playa del Inglés

Holidaymakers choosing Playa del Inglés as their base will probably find that, apart from price, four major factors will determine their selection of accommodation: proximity to the beach, proximity to the sand dunes, proximity to the night life, and in winter the availability of a heated swimming pool. Virtually no one will be far from a bus route: the stop at Plaza de Maspalomas (opposite the Joy nightclub entrance) is the closest to the beach.

Night life is a different matter, as all bus services in the area, except the infrequent Las Palmas-Maspalomas 05 night bus, terminate shortly after 9pm. A central position, within easy walking distance of the Yumbo Centrum would probably be ideal for night birds. Taxis, of course, operate all night, but repeated use of them in the early hours of the morning, even for quite short distances, can eat into the holiday pesetas.

AIRPORT & LAS PALMAS →

N
W E
S

AUTOPISTA

SAN AGUSTIN

BAHIA FELIZ

Casino Palace Nightclub

Centro Commercial Morru Besudo & Bus Station

Playa de Aguila

Playa de Tarajalillo

Carretera 812

Playa de Morro Besudo

Centro Commercial San Agustín

Playa de San Agustín

namar

SOUTH-EAST COAST RESORTS

The shoreline to the north of San Agustin

attended before midnight. The appearance of leather-clad men with bristling moustaches and shaven heads indicates the concentrated presence around the north-east corner, at all levels, of the south coast's gay bars.

Although Playa del Inglés has no real centre, at night, the paved area facing the **Ecumenical Church of San Salvador** does provide an assembly point of sorts. The curved, aircraft-hangar form of the church provides the only architectural relief from straight lines to be seen in the town. Discos and shops abound in the **Kasbah** and **Metro** centres, which lie beside the church, and a lively atmosphere prevails.

At Playa del Inglés, the coastal promenade is officially named **Paseo Costa Canaria** and this leads to the southern tip of the town, where the Riu Palace Hotel overlooks the famous sand dunes. It is much quicker to approach the dunes via this promenade than to follow the crocodile of holidaymakers that march towards them along the shoreline, splashing their feet from time to time in the water.

Nowadays, the sand dunes, which are indigenous, begin at the point of the triangle that marks the southerly extent of the built-up area of Playa del Inglés, but they once extended further inland, until removed by the developers. Photographs of Las Palmas show that similar sand dunes existed at the northern end of the island until the 1950s. However, no trace of them remains.

SAN FERNANDO

Although technically part of Maspalomas, this quarter, laid out to accommodate Canarios working in the resorts, has such a completely different atmosphere that it is better treated as a separate entity. Most will approach it from Cruce de la Viude de Franco, the large roundabout straddling the *carretera* at the north end of Avenida de Tirajana; the 72 bus links the quarter with most of Playa del Inglés (but mornings only), and the more direct 31 bus, which follows the *carretera*, by-passing most of Playa del Inglés, is even more convenient for some.

Unappealing blocks of apartments and offices are all that can be seen from the south side of the *carretera*, giving the impression that San Fernando has made desperate attempts to dissuade tourists from visiting it. Ignore these, for behind lies an extremely attractive housing estate, by far the most enjoyable

Centro Commercial in the south, and two *supermercado's* that are geared to local rather than north European tastes and incomes. There are also genuine *tapas* bars – or at least as genuine as the rather limited shellfish found in Canary waters permits, and several restaurants offer traditional Canary dishes. It is well worth crossing the *carretera* to visit the 'real Spain'.

Overlooking the Cruz de la Viude de Franco roundabout, is the eponymous old-established Canary restaurant transferred to its present site from smaller but more picturesque premises some years ago; surprisingly, the original building still remains on the west side of the roundabout, surrounded by an unkempt garden.

Refreshingly intimate in scale without being too small, the shopping centre of San Fernando appeals mainly because it is, in essence, a village high street, which actually incorporates shops selling goods

Good value supermarkets

Soon after arriving in the south, a visit to either of San Fernando's supermarkets **Ansoco**, or behind it, **Hiperdino**, is strongly recommended. Load up with as much as possible, and invest in a taxi for the return journey. Even those who are not self-catering will find that the prices of alcohol, soft drinks, biscuits and confectionery are much lower here than at most other places in the south, and there is also a wide range of Spanish charcuterie and cheeses: great for lunchtime sandwiches.

that people living there need. Differences between this centre and the entirely tourist-inspired versions along the coast are really quite subtle, but the overall ambience is incomparably more natural, human – and Spanish. In the main street, reached by steps, La Bodeguita del Medio is probably the best *tapas* bar in the area, and an excellent spot for lunch – go easy on the drinks, however, which are very much cheaper than in tourist land.

In the same street as **Hiperdino** (see box on opposite page) **Los Josés – la Tapita** is an economically-priced restaurant.

Pepe el Breca, on the main road to Fataga, is generally regarded as the best (and most expensive) of San Fernando's restaurants.

MASPALOMAS

Simply meaning 'more pigeons', Maspalomas refers to the migrating

A lighthouse, oasis and sand dunes

On their first visit to Maspalomas, most make for the ancient lighthouse, which remains the south coast's one important landmark. It is not apparent where the beach of Maspalomas joins that of Playa del Inglés, almost the entire stretch being lined with virtually identical sunbeds and parasols, which double as useful windbreaks. On the east side of the lighthouse is the still picturesque oasis of **Charca de Maspalomas**, the edges of its lagoon fringed with feathery pampas grass. Behind this rise the first of the sand dunes. The walk across them to the southern tip of Playa del Inglés may not appear to be long, but at least an hour should be allowed, as feet sink tiringly in the sand, even if the larger dunes are avoided.

As may be expected, camel rides provide a popular 'mini Sahara' trip among the dunes, and make good souvenir photographs. There is even a camel safari from the Maspalomas sand dunes into the mountains, as far as Arteara and Fataga.

The great Maspalomas sand dunes are at their most tranquil in the early evening or morning

birds – not only pigeons – that take a break on the lagoon of the Maspalomas oasis before continuing their journey from Europe to their winter quarters. Officially, the name Maspalomas also covers Playa del Inglés and San Fernando, but to visitors it denotes only the area around the *faro* (lighthouse), the lagoon and the sand dunes.

Until the mid-1950s, Maspalomas was a centre for tomato growing: the ever-present sunshine and absence of frosts ensured all-year-round crops. Tourism, however, proved to be more profitable, and three luxury-grade hotels now stand where tomatoes formerly ripened. One of these hotels, the Maspalomas Oasis, has retained its five-star rating for many years. During the day, masses of holidaymakers, supplemented on Sundays by Las Palmas sun-worshippers, trek from the bus terminal at Plaza del Faro to the beach. The *paseo* is lined with souvenir shops and restaurants – prices are surprisingly reasonable.

Nude sunbathing is officially permitted in the dunes away from the beach and also in a designated section of **Playa de las Mujeres,** west of the lighthouse, where most of the nudists are German. Many Germans have an ingrained belief that to give an airing to parts of the body that do not normally get one is a good and healthy thing to do. It is fairly apparent, from what is on view, that vanity can have little part to play in their enthusiasm; those who have ever suffered traumas after accidentally surprising grandma in the bath might be advised to give both the dunes and the designated areas a wide berth!

West from the lighthouse, the beach becomes dangerous, due to the occasional whirlpools that form a short distance out to sea: swimmers should avoid the area.

Additional Information

ACCOMMODATION

Don Miguel Hotel ***
30 Avenida Tirajana,
Playa del Inglés
☎ 928 761508, Fax 928 771904

Ifa Dunamar Hotel ****
8 Helsinki,
Playa del Inglés
☎ 928 772800, Fax 928 773465

Maspalomas Oasis Hotel *****
Playa de Maspalomas
☎ 928 141448, Fax 928 141192

Meliá Tamarindos Hotel *****
3 Retama,
San Agustín
☎ 928 774090, Fax 928 774091

EATING OUT

Pepe el Breca
Carratera de Fataga
☎ 928 772637
Open daily: 1-4pm, 8pm to midnight.

THINGS TO DO

Fataga Camel Safari
Barranco de Arteara 5-7,
Fataga
☎ 928 798686 or 928 798698

TOURIST INFORMATION OFFICE

Yumbo Centrum
Playa del Inglés
☎ 928 762591, or 928 771550
Fax 928 767848
Open: October to June, Monday to Friday 9am-9pm, Saturday 9am-1pm.

LAS MELONERAS

Soon after passing Faro de Maspalomas, a path stretches westward above the cliffs in the direction of Playa de las Meloneras. Below lie strangely-shaped rocks, which are much favoured by sunbathers. Gradually, the path veers northward and, after a 25-minute walk, a descent can be made to the small beach of Las Meloneras. Protection from east and north winds is given by the surrounding hills, and there is a popular beachfront restaurant, **Casa Serafin**, from where sunbeds and parasols may be hired. Nudism is permitted at the south end of the bay.

PASITO BLANCO

The main coastal road continues westward; those with private vehicles

in search of very secluded sunbathing can turn left and follow an unpaved track to a 500m (550yd) long beach of fine, clean sand at **El Hornillo**.

Pasito Blanco's marina, also reached by a side road, gives added protection to the small cove in which its beach is set, and the water is therefore calmer and clearer than usual around this coast: it is, in consequence, popular with scuba divers. An extensive camping park behind the marina, rare in the Canaries, provides virtually all the local accommodation.

West of Pasito Blanco's headland, the long Santa Agueda Bay is spoiled by its cement works.

ARGUINEGUÍN

Many will be tempted to visit Arguineguín, as this is the only example of a genuine fishing village on the coast between San Agustín and Puerto de Mogán. Arguineguín's *tapas* bars are excellent – look for **Bar Fanie** – and the port can be lively. As may be expected, the local restaurants are renowned for the freshness and quality of the fish served. A large, open-air market is held every Tuesday morning.

PATALAVACA

Patalavaca developed behind a small jetty from which tomatoes were formerly shipped to Las Palmas, connections by road then being extremely tortuous. Now, the town almost entirely comprises apartment blocks, occupied by Scandinavian holidaymakers. The coastal promenade between Arguineguín and Patalavaca is most pleasant. Patalavaca's chief attraction lies in its clean beach, the sand being unusually pale for the area.

'Anfi' Beach

A fifteen-minute walk from Patalavaca, this beach fronts the luxurious Anfi time-share development, which is well-worth visiting in its own right. Gleaming-white coral sand was brought by tanker from Jamaican waters, and coconut palms have been planted around it. This is undoubtedly the island's most 'tropical' beach, and all may use its facilities. Not to be missed.

PUERTO RICO

It is only a short distance along the main road to Puerto Rico, but don't try to walk it. The road enters a tunnel and then, at its end, a superb view of the favourite resort of the British in Gran Canaria is revealed. An even more dramatic approach can be made by sea, either from Arguineguín or Puerto de Mogán, but few make their initial contact with Puerto Rico in this way. Puerto Rico means rich port, which it certainly never was until the possibilities of its micro-climate – significantly more annual sunshine than Playa del Inglés – and its protection from most winds by embracing hills, suggested tourist development.

Although there is a delightful *apartotel*, almost all the accommodation in Puerto Rico is self-catering, tariffs in general falling with the altitude of the building occupied. Tour operators offer some amazingly cheap package tours to the resort from the UK in winter outside the Christmas/New Year period, but almost all of them perch their clients in the very highest located buildings – great views but an arduous approach. Buses wind up the steep hillsides at fairly regular intervals (although not at night). However, the fittest generally walk down (hoping that something vital – such as money – has not been forgotten) and return by taxi.

With its concentration on low-cost self-catering apartments and a safe beach of golden sand, Puerto Rico is primarily aimed at young families and far more children will be seen

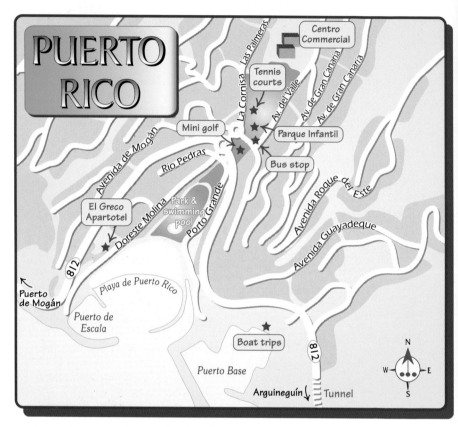

PUERTO RICO

here than anywhere else in the Canaries. In consequence, the night life is extremely limited.

Buses connect Las Palmas and all the intervening coastal resorts with Puerto Rico, depositing visitors in the town centre; most then immediately make their way through the adjacent park to the beach. This is a unique and most praiseworthy feature of the town, incorporating children's play areas, tennis courts and many examples of Canarian flora. The mature trees provide a welcoming splash of green, which is unmatched by the other south coast resorts.

Between the park and the beach, a delightful open-air swimming pool complex is popular with those whose accommodation includes no pool. In winter the water is actually heated sufficiently for almost all – not just

Puerto Rico's development

To overcome the lack of an attractive beach tons of golden sand were imported from the Sahara Desert in tankers. A new road to Playa del Inglés and thence to the airport and Las Palmas was laid out, and the developers moved in. Unfortunately, flat land was limited, and gradually, with no obvious restrictions imposed, white apartment blocks climbed up the hillsides. From the centre of the town, it is rather like being on stage in an Ancient Greek amphitheatre of gigantic proportions.

Boats moor well away from Puerto Rico's beach

masochists – to swim in: a rare event in the Canaries. Daily or weekly tickets are available.

Boat trips

Boat services are run at half-hourly intervals by Lineas Salmon to Puerto de Mogán or Arguineguín (return fares only) from the jetty, south of the beach. It is well worth taking both trips on separate days, although the former is rather more spectacular – look out for enormous caves in the volcanic cliffs.

The town's southern port can be reached by walking across the attractive pedestrian bridge over the tidal stream, which skirts the east side of the beach. From here, departing at 10.30am, a whole day cruise can be made on the red-sailed windjammer *San Miguel*, with lunch included. Motorised vessels also offer shark-fishing excursions further out to sea. If the sea is calm, trips are made to Güigüi beach, the island's most secluded, where a barbecue lunch is provided.

Back in the town centre, just behind the park, is the **Centro Commercial** of Puerto Rico. This exceptionally dismal concrete development accommodates the resort's shops and entertainment facilities. Here also are located the most ambitious of Puerto Rico's restaurants (evenings only).

While those staying in Puerto Rico are unlikely to find its protected beach windswept, the sea water in winter is no warmer than elsewhere on the island. Due to the smaller units built and lower prices charged, much of the accommodation in Puerto Rico does not include a swimming pool. The top spot to stay is the El Greco Apartotel, sited at beach level, which does have a large pool, as well as maid service and restaurants; bookings must always be made in advance via a tour operator.

PUERTO DE MOGÁN

The 812 road from Puerto Rico to Puerto de Mogán skirts **Playa de las Amadores**, winding close to the shore, and providing occasional glimpses of small bays, some with tourist developments completed or underway, the most important of which are **Playa de Tauro** and **Playa**

del Cura. Overlooking the former, the camping site of Guantánamo, with a capacity of 150, is the largest on the island. As has already been indicated, a return boat trip from either Puerto Rico or Arguineguín is the most impressive way to arrive at this delightful resort, with its dramatic background of the lush, steeply-rising Barranco de Mogán. At Puerto de Mogán, unusual in the Canaries, the marina has undoubtedly enhanced the village.

Just about everything seems right: low-rise buildings, mostly serving as self-catering units, have been laid out along the banks of narrow canals, linked by Venetian-style bridges (the architect was Italian). The walls of the buildings have been smothered with flowers, and exotic plants grow in small garden plots; arches pretending to act as buttresses span the walkways.

In 2000, much luxury development was taking place immediately behind the small, grey sand beach,

Puerto de Mogán, designed in traditional style, is reminiscent of a Spanish fishing village on the Atlantic coast

which will almost certainly be improved when the new apartments and shops have been opened. Already, prices at the resort have escalated to become the highest in the Canaries, a reflexion of its outstanding attractiveness.

Most will wander, initially, around the marina's canals, revelling in the shops, bars and restaurants, which are located in a refreshing, higgledy-piggledy way. Day-trippers naturally come at all times but particularly on Fridays for the weekly market, when the resort can be uncomfortably crowded. The marina was built in front of an existing fishing port, on reclaimed land, and the original buildings were left untouched. Behind the waterfront restaurants it is pleasant to climb the narrow streets of old Puerto de Mogán to the mirador, with its spectacular views. Unfortunately, the old village no longer has a bar or restaurant.

Sol Club de Mar operates the holidaymaker's apartments on the marina as well as the superbly located hotel to the south of it, from which there are exquisite views across the bay towards the headland. The hotel's swimming pool complex, which is most elegant, may also be used by those staying in the apartments, as may also the hotel's other facilities, which include an excellent restaurant. As Puerto Mogán's sunshine record is said to be even better than Puerto Rico's, those seeking a relaxing holiday amidst idyllic surroundings, without insisting on a golden beach or swinging discos, will find Puerto de Mogán hard to match anywhere in the Canary Islands.

Submarine trip

Lineas Salmon's boat trips along the coast pick up and deposit passengers at the southerly point of the harbour but, on the opposite jetty, near the lighthouse, is docked the *Yellow Submarine*, a vessel manufactured in Finland in 1988 specifically for viewing marine life. Apprehensive voyagers are lulled by soft music as the boat sinks slowly below sea level. An instant 'coral reef' has been created by sinking a wreck, which is popular as a hideaway for smaller fish as it provides a refuge from large predators. The trip lasts approximately 45 minutes – the cost of tickets, however, is not inconsiderable. For those booking a trip on the *Yellow Submarine* in advance there is a free bus service from Puerto Rico and the major hotels in Playa del Inglés.

Additional Information

ACCOMMODATION

El Greco Apartotel AT
Puerto Chico,
Puerto Rico
☎ 928 749214

Sol Club de Mar Hotel*
Puerto de Mogán
☎ 928 565066

EATING OUT

Oliver
Shopping Centre,
Puerto Rico
Open: 6.30-10.30pm (not Tuesdays).

Tu Casa
Puerto de Mogán
Open: 12 noon-midnight (not Tuesdays).

Jack el Negro
Puerto de Mogán
Open: 6pm (not Mondays))
(speciality wood-fired grills).

BOAT TRIPS

Lineas Salmon
Leaves Puerto Rico for Puerto de Mogán hourly 11am to 4pm (45 minutes); for Arguineguín hourly 10.30am to 4.30pm (45 minutes).
Check times locally.

Yellow Submarine
Puerto de Mogán
☎ 928 565108/565048 for reservation and free bus.

TOURIST OFFICE

Shopping Centre Puerto Rico
☎ 928 560099

A wide variety of fruit and vegetables is grown on Gran Canaria – harvesting aubergine in the Mogán Valley

Itineraries in the South

The following itineraries, all beginning and ending at the south coast resorts, have been selected bearing in mind that the majority of holidaymakers may not have the use of a motor vehicle. Unless specifically mentioned all locations may be reached by bus.

Resorts along the south coast have been described in a clockwise direction, ending at Puerto de Mogán; however all the following excursions, which can be made from any of them, will be described in anti-clockwise order from Puerto de Mogán, ending north of San Agustín. Holidaymakers based at Las Palmas will find it easier and quicker to explore the central mountain range from there rather than from the south.

Due to the terrain, most hiking expeditions in Gran Canaria tend to become rather strenuous affairs once the roads have been left. For enthusiastic walkers, a great deal of advice regarding clothing and detailed topographical features is essential. Such advice, outside the scope of this book, is given in *Landscapes of Gran Canaria* by Noel Rochford, published by Sunflower Books.

THE WESTERN BARRANCOS & COAST

The 810 road from Puerto de Mogán connects the locations on this itinerary, and is followed by the 38 bus from Las Palmas, which may be joined at San Agustín or San Fernando, but not at Playa del Inglés, as it keeps to the *carretera*. Buses 84 and 86 link Puerto de Mogán with Mogán. However, if a taxi is required at Mogán, it must be hired from Puerto de Mogán.

Mogán Pueblo & its *barranco*

The elevated *pueblo* (village) of Mogán, after which the now much larger port is named, has inevitably been affected by tourism, and establishments offering souvenirs and the usual 'international' dishes have proliferated. However, it is still attractive and certainly worth a halt.

The 810 follows the Mogán valley, one of the most fertile and beautiful in Gran Canaria. Here will be found aubergines, papayas, avocados, mangoes and coffee in abundance. It seems strange that the almost rainless port should be located so near to this well-watered region, but clouds will often begin to appear as the mountain peak rising behind Mogán are approached, and heavy showers regularly develop, particularly on winter afternoons, filling the ducted streams which irrigate the valley.

The green upper reaches of the ravine are so idyllic that, on their return journey to the coast, many bus passengers are tempted to explore them on foot by alighting at Mogán and walking downhill to Puerto de Mogán (9km/6 miles). Unfortunately, there are no public footpaths, the land on either side of the road being divided into numerous small-holdings, many of which are defended by barking dogs. Although none of the animals will be rabid, their apparent ferocity can be alarming, and there have been occasional reports of intrepid tourists being bitten. It is

In the foothills south-west of the central mountains, Gran Canaria's reservoirs (presas) are all man made

Pie de la Cuesta

This hamlet stands at the head of the Mogán valley, its small restaurant, El Aurillo, retaining a Canarian ambience. For those with (preferably four-wheel-drive) vehicles, and strong nerves, the extremely narrow 811, right, leads north-eastward. The lower reaches of the road, shortly after Pie de la Cuesta has been passed, zig-zag steeply and develop into an unsurfaced track with precipitous drops. Despite being shown as a good road on some maps, the planned upgrading awaits completion. The track passes between two reservoirs with spectacular views, before improving and eventually meeting up with the 815, which penetrates the dramatic central heights of the island and is best approached from the north.

better to view the exotic crops from the road, preferably the terrace of the Acaymo restaurant, which overlooks the ravine to the south of Mogán and is considered one of the best in the region.

Veneguera & its *barranco*

Most, however, will opt to proceed westward in the direction of San Nicolás after leaving Pie de la Cuesta

(see box above). The Barranco de Veneguera soon stretches towards the coast, and a side road, the 10.2, branches off to **Veneguera** village, a small cluster of Moorish-style white houses at the *barranco's* head. Unfortunately, this road soon becomes little more than a track – do not believe the wildly over-optimistic maps – and a four-wheel-drive vehicle is needed to follow the *barranco* to **Playa de Veneguera** in comfort.

The remote valley of Veneguera is remarkable for the abundance of candelabra cacti (*cardón*), evocative of an American Wild West film.

Los Azulejos

The 810 continues northward from Veneguera village to Tasarte, and there are great views of Los Azulejos from this stretch. Not only geologists will be impressed by the famous multi-coloured strata, which betrays the volcanic origin of the mountains. Predominant colours are pastel green and pink, but other hues also make an appearance; no-where else in the Canaries is such mineral exuberance displayed.

Two more valleys now swing away westward towards the coast; they are named after their respective villages,

Tasarte and **Tasartico**. (See the west coast beaches section.)

San Nicolás de Tolentino
(Aldea de San Nicolás)

After the Tasartico branch road has been passed, the 810 descends to the market town of San Nicolás de Tolentino, lying in the wide valley of the Barranco Aldea. There is not a great deal to see here, even though passing tourists are catered for. As in much of southern Spain, extensive plastic sheeting has been stretched over the tomatoes, which increases the yield, but at the expense of gravely disfiguring the environment; few will wish to trek through this weird landscape. The town is alternatively referred to as Aldea de San Nicolás.

Puerto de la Aldea

Most visitors will soon continue the short distance from San Nicolás to

Puerto de la Aldea

Fiesta del Charco

Every September, the local community of Puerto de Aldea converges on the port to take part in the Fiesta del Charco, casting palm leaves into the sea to ensure good crops the following year.

Puerto de la Aldea, a peaceful fishing harbour with a small, dark-sand beach protected by cliffs. Look out for **Peñon Bermejo**, a vase-shaped rock. It was at Puerto de la Aldea that the fossilised remains of the Verdino dog, over 2,000 years old, were discovered.

Bus 115 runs between San Nicolás and Puerto de la Aldea (but not very frequently) and bus 101, which ends its north coast journey from Las Palmas at San Nicolás, goes most of the way to it, but keeps to the 810; it is also a very restricted service. Taxis can easily be hired at San Nicolás, but only with some difficulty at Puerto de la Aldea.

Those without their own transport who wish to proceed further along the north coast are recommended not to be too ambitious in one day. No further than Puerto de la Aldea, should be attempted if returning southward by the 38 bus. It is, of course, possible to return to the south coast via Las Palmas if preferred – a much longer journey in distance although not in time, particularly if a south-east rather than a south-west coast resort is the final destination. Details of the northward continuation from San Nicolás via Las Palmas are given on pages 83-87.

THE WEST COAST BEACHES

Tasarte & Asno Beaches

Northwards from Puerto de Mogán, there is no coastal road northward until Puerto de la Aldea is reached. However, as already noted, narrow side roads, the 16.3 and the 16.5 respectively, branch off the 810, and follow the *barrancos* of Tasarte and Tasartico, providing motor access to the small, secluded beaches of Tasarte and Asno, both of which comprise grey sand with some gravel. Bus 86 from Playa del Inglés follows the 810 in the direction of San Nicolás, and then branches left at Tasarte, continuing to its beach. Even smaller and more secluded beaches exist, but these can be reached only by experienced hikers or by boat.

Güigüi Beach

In calm weather, boats depart from Puerto Rico to Güigüi, considered to be the most appealing of all the remote beaches on this part of the coast. It can be reached only by boat and is overlooked by jagged peaks, there are absolutely no facilities; organisers of the trip therefore provide a picnic lunch, which is included in the excursion price. The coastline passed is most dramatic, consisting of mountain ridges punctuated by ravines – and nothing else – no ports and, once Playa de Veneguera has been passed, little sign of any human presence. It is virgin Canary coastline, unmatched elsewhere on the island. A word of warning to poor sailors – the seas can be rough.

PARKS & ACTIVITIES

Palmitos Park

A visit to Palmitos Park, with the possible exception of a trip to Las Palmas, is the most popular of all the excursions from the southern resorts – and understandably so. Bus 45 runs from San Agustín via Playa del Inglés, and bus 70 from Puerto Rico, via Faro de Maspalomas to the park. The stops served bear the legend 'Palmitos Park Bus', but other buses also use them. Covering 200,000 sq m (240,000sq yd), the park, predominantly an aviary, is set at the head of the steep Barranco de Chamoriscán; a reservoir is located not far to the west, and springs and pools abound within the reservation. There are now estimated to be around 1,500 exotic birds from all parts of the world on view in the park, one-third of them flying freely; 230 different species are represented. Try not to miss the free 25-minute show (eight per day) given by macaws, which have been trained to perform extraordinary tricks.

Almost as impressive as the birds is the sub-tropical vegetation, equally international in nature, which includes towering cacti and fifty-one types of palm tree. Exotic blooms are displayed in the Orchid House. Within the Tropical Butterfly House, Europe's largest, hundreds of butterflies and moths fly freely.

Palmitos Park boasts exotic birds, orchids, butterflies and an extensive cacti garden

Ocean Park

On the 70 bus route is Ocean Park, a water park aimed at families with young children: the usual water toboggans and splashing spectaculars are a delight to youngsters (who are admitted at half price). The 66 bus from the airport drops at Ocean Park immediately before its terminus at Faro 2 shopping centre.

Tarajalillo Go-karting

At this recently opened centre mini tracks and mini vehicles have been designed so that even the under-fives can participate in go-carting with complete safety. For those over ten years old, there are specially designed mini motorbikes. It is located at the north end of the San Agustín complex, close to the private airport.

Sioux City

After a 'paella' Western film had been shot on the Cañón del Aguila, a steep-sided ravine running inland from just to the north of San Agustín, it was decided that the set should be retained. This has since been developed as a tourist attraction, and Wild West shows are held.

Sioux City is open most of the day (not Monday), with continuous shows taking place in the square. The greatest appeal is to youngsters (plus Wild West enthusiasts), who can enter the village shops, bars, hotel and church. Lunch and dinner are served in the Three Stars Saloon and the BBQ. Daytime shows include can-can dancers, a bank hold-up, a shootout between villains and the sheriff's men, knife-throwing, lassoing, and cattle-herding.

Throughout the year on Friday nights (more frequently in summer), at 8pm, a Wild West show and barbecue dinner is held. Bus 29 runs from Faro de Maspalomas to Sioux City via Playa del Inglés and San Agustín from 11am, but the hourly night bus, 05, from Morro Besudo, or private transport will be needed to return from the barbecue, which ends at midnight.

TOWARDS THE HIGH MOUNTAINS

This excursion follows the Carretera de Fataga (road 12.1) from Playa del Inglés, a continuation of Avenida de Tirajana. Bus 48 makes the 6km (3.7 miles) journey to Mundo Aborigen.

Mundo Aborigen

Mundo Aborigen (Native World), of which the Canarios are very proud, is an open-air museum depicting the life of the island's original inhabitants, the Guanches. The museum, spread over a hillside, primarily consists of wax or wooden models of Guanches doing useful things. Opened in 1994, it is now an established attraction for those with an interest in the archipelago's history, and particularly local children on school outings.

The 18 bus, which starts at San Fernando – outside the pharmacy in Avenida de Tirajana just after this has emerged from the north side of the Carretera del Sur – continues northward to Fataga, San Bartolomé de Tirajana and Ayacata.

Wax models at Mundo Aborigen open-air museum depict the daily life of the Guanches – the original inhabitants of Gran Canaria

Fataga

The Barranco de Fataga, climbing ever upward from San Fernando to San Bartolomé de Tirajana is, for much of its length, one of the most dramatic and vertiginous in Gran Canaria. Some find the short stretch as far as Mundo Aborigen exciting enough, but it is after this that the hairs on the back of the neck stand on end, the mouth goes dry, and one thinks fondly of the folks back home. Surely, no vehicle can negotiate that bend! How could any approaching car avoid head-on contact? The sheer drop must be over 300m (1,000ft) – and there are no protective walls! The shrill screams of tourists on the bus give great amusement to the locals, many of whom travel for much of the route at least twice a day without even bothering to glance out of the window. Sufferers from vertigo have been warned!

Sited on a low hill rising from the floor of the *barranco*, Fataga is a delight. Dark blocks of volcanic stone are revealed in the walls of the houses, thus enlivening the white plasterwork, a typical Canary feature. Most of the village lies on the west side of the main road, its cobbled streets winding around the occasional small-holding. Unlike Playa del Inglés, the name of even the shortest thoroughfare is proudly displayed. A large restaurant on the main road caters primarily for tourists, its prices and 'international' menus rivalling those along the coastal strip. Opposite this, however, is the village bar, its daily *tapas* menu chalked on a board. Bus passengers will arrive at Fataga around lunchtime, and many of them will wish to spend some time at the bar or restaurant before exploring the village (establish with certainty the return bus times).

Located a short distance both to the south and north of Fataga are camel safari centres, where beasts may be hired for accompanied treks of varying length through the valley.

San Bartolomé de Tirajana

It is possible for those without a hire car to continue by number 18 bus to the not very exciting small town of San Bartolomé de Tirajana (or Tunte), which is encircled by mountains. Although this is the administrative centre of a huge area, including much of the tourist coastline, there is nothing of exceptional architectural interest to be seen even though San Bartolomé's church has reopened to visitors after extensive restoration. Roads leading to a *mirador* are signposted, but the views, although pleasant, hardly seem worth a pedestrian's effort. The local *parador*, which has seen better days, even though the food is still quite good, offers a splendid view of the Tirajana crater. On the main road, near the bus stop, Bar Martini serves *guindilla*, a local aperitif, which evokes a sweet Fernet Branca. Bar Sergio, nearby, is more adventurous in its selection of *tapas*.

Those returning to San Fernando will approach the end of their hair-raising journey with tranquil views of the Maspalomas coast, dominated by the lighthouse and the sand dunes.

Motorists can continue from San Bartolomé into the high central mountain range of Gran Canaria, an excursion which is described next. Non-motorists wishing to make the same trip have three alternatives: wait until Sunday morning's 8am departure of the 18 bus from San Fernando, travel via Las Palmas or take an escorted tour.

San Bartolomé de Tirajana

THE CENTRAL MOUNTAINS

All those spending their first holiday in Gran Canaria are urged to visit the dramatic range of mountains that occupies most of its centre. Like Tenerife's snow-covered Teide, the range is volcanic in origin, although no similar dramatic cone dominates. This has the visual effect of making Gran Canaria appear to be, erroneously, a larger island than Tenerife, where it is quite difficult to get away from the omnipresent views of its towering mountain. In clear weather, Teide can be seen from much of the north coast and the central mountains of Gran Canaria. Although it rises out of the sea in a faintly menacing way, the volcano's last eruption of any importance was in 1789.

Round-the-island coach tours include the central mountains in their itineraries, but these have several drawbacks: most halt at very touristy restaurants (the price of an indifferent lunch usually being included in the package) and all spend far too much time in souvenir shops, risibly described as *artesanas* (craft shops). Almost all these huge emporiums are located far from anywhere of interest, and the poor holidaymaker is trapped – the only alternative is usually to stubbornly remain seated in the coach and read a good book.

Another intrinsic drawback of coach tours, particularly frustrating to photographers, is that stops can be made only where they have been scheduled by the operator, and there are few of them; those travelling by public transport, although dependant on bus stops, will be less restricted.

Ayacata

At San Bartolomé de Tirajana, the 815 continues its climb westward towards the island's highest peaks,

Mountain weather watch

The weather in the mountains is extremely fickle: on the south coast the sun may well be shining brightly out of a clear blue sky, while mist or torrential rain is blotting out everything from view on the heights, just a few miles distant. In general, a morning start – as early as possible – is recommended, because cloud tends to build up from around mid-day. Those who have pre-booked either their coach tour or hire car will, of course, have to accept whatever the weather brings but, if at all possible, the mountains should be avoided in overcast conditions as so little can then be seen. A local radio programme gives weather forecasts in English every morning.

crossing the pass of **Cruz Grande** (1,200m/3,940ft); at Ayacata the road becomes the 811. Nestling at *(cont'd on page 54)*

Roque Nueblo, a dramatic basalt monolith – the world's highest, has become the symbol of Gran Canaria

the foot of the mountains, the small village of Ayacata serves as the terminal point for some of the number 18 buses, which leave San Fernando, Sunday to Friday at 8am. On Sunday this continues to **Cruz de Tejeda**, the best-known viewpoint in the mountain range, but from here, unfortunately, the return bus leaves as early as 12.30pm. It is essential that bus

Roques Nublo & Bentaiga

Towering high above Ayacata, immediately to the north, at 1,803m (5,914ft) above sea level, **Roque Nublo** (Cloud Rock), the loftiest basalt monolith in the world, points skyward from its platform. Although this is not quite the highest point in Gran Canaria, the rock's dramatic appearance has made it the symbol of the island. Some think that Roque Nublo was formed by the Guanches, who appear to have regarded it as sacred, but the shape has been created entirely by climatic erosion. Little vegetation gains a foothold in this rocky landscape, where the effect of wind and rain has created a barren wilderness punctuated by other rock formations, which are similar to, although less dominating than, Roque Nublo's.

The 811 to Cruz de Tejeda skirts a great plateau after climbing the ridge above Ayacata. To the west can be seen **Roque Bentaiga**, which motorists may approach more closely by following the track to the left from the point where the main road does an abrupt right turn: there is a car park below. This monolithic rock was also sacred to the Guanches, many of whom lived in the Guayve caves at its base.

Roque Bentaiga dominates the surrounding landscape

passengers obtain up-to-date information on this route's timetable as the service is limited. Set amidst a very rocky terrain, Ayacata is a particularly attractive sight late January to February, when the almond trees are in blossom.

Tejeda & Cruz de Tejeda

Tejeda, nestling in its valley, is the terminus for bus 305, from Las Palmas via Santa Brígida. Those without their own transport, who wish to spend longer in the mountains than the departure time of the last 18 bus to San Fernando permits, may prefer to return to the south coast by this bus (via Las Palmas), leaving Tejeda in the late afternoon – a daily service. Marzipan figures, almonds, honey and *bienmesabes*, a speciality cake, are made and sold in the village.

Cruz de Tejeda, on a bend in the road 3km (2 miles) north of Tejeda village, is regarded as marking the centre of Gran Canaria. It is so-named from its cross (*cruz*), now of stone but originally made of wood, which stands in the small plaza overlooked by the newly restored Parador Nacional de Tejeda.

Although, as mentioned earlier, there is a limited bus service from the south, all points north of Tejeda are more easily reached by bus passengers from Las Palmas (bus 305). The slopes here are heavily wooded with pine trees, but from gaps between them can be gained the most famous view on the island – Roque Bentaiga to the left, and ahead, in the distance, Tenerife's Mount Teide, which gleams spectacularly after a winter snowfall. Unless the weather is poor, many will wish to indulge in a ramble, but remember that Cruz de Tejeda is 1,450m

(4,800ft) above sea level, and therefore normally chilly, particularly when low cloud envelops it in damp mist: warm clothing should always be taken as a precaution against abrupt falls in temperature.

Los Pechos & Pozo de las Nieves

Experienced hikers can, theoretically, trek to the highest point on Gran Canaria, known as Los Pechos (the peaks) or alternatively **Pico de las Nieves** (Peak of the Snows), at 1,949m (6,393ft) above sea level, but motorists can approach it by road directly from Cruz de Tejeda. The main 811 road is followed eastward (in the direction of Las Palmas) and the first turn right, the 15.3, then taken. At the cross-roads turn left on the 18.3 in the direction of Telde and then first right. The entire route cuts through an ancient forest of Canary pines.

As a military radio station has been built on Los Pechos, it is more rewarding to continue to the end of the road, which ascends much of the nearby 1,864m (6,114ft) high **Pozo de las Nieves**: a scramble to the summit is not too difficult. The name of this mountain, meaning Pit of the Snows, is a reference to an ice storage pit that was once excavated on its north side, it has nothing to do with the snows of Tenerife's Mount Teide as many surmise.

For those returning to the south coast, the quickest route is to take the road towards Ayacata, turning left at the cross roads (the 17.6), and then left again, on the 815 to San Bartolomé. If wishing to return to Las Palmas, the right turn at the same cross roads (the 15.3) should be taken; this soon joins the 811, right, to San Mateo, Santa Brígida (see page 94) and Las Palmas.

TELDE

From the south, Telde can best be visited on route to or from nearby Las Palmas. There are many buses to Las Palmas, and the hourly bus 90 links Telde directly with the southern resorts.

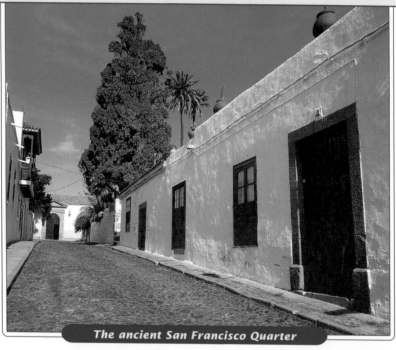

The ancient San Francisco Quarter

Telde is unfairly neglected by most visitors to Gran Canaria. Much of the city is relatively modern and without interest, but the ancient core has been almost completely preserved. Perhaps nowhere else on the island can the thrust of early colonialism be felt so strongly. The Guanches had certainly favoured the area, two of their largest settlements in Gran Canaria, *Tara* and *Cendro*, being located here. It is said that the renowned Guanche ruler, King Doramas, established his court near the present Telde. In the fourteenth century, Telde became the first bishopric in the Canary Islands. Like **Agüimes** and **Ingenio**, its wealth had depended on sugar cane, and Telde's economy collapsed when American-produced sugar took over in the mid-sixteenth century: fewer than 1,000 were living in the town by 1700.

Church of San Juan Bautista

The chief monument of Telde is its church of **San Juan Bautista** (St John the Baptist), dating from the late fifteenth century, and still dominating the plaza that bears its name. Externally, the porch is genuine fifteenth-century Gothic work, but the twin towers are relatively modern additions, albeit in the Gothic style.

Internally, the coffered ceilings of the north chapels are *mudéjar* work, a style evolved by Moorish Christian 'converts' in Spain. It is known that Moors were among those engaged in the arduous work of cane-cutting at Telde, and they may have influenced this feature.

The pointed arch of the chancel is a rare late-Gothic example in the islands. Within the chancel are two of the most important artistic treasures to be found in the Canaries. Embellishing the high altar is a figure of Christ, sculpted from the compressed leaves and roots of maize; it is attributed to the skill of Mexican Indians from the state of Tabasco. Even more important, to the south of this, displayed within an enormous glass case, is a carved and gilded wooden altarpiece, which is contemporary with the church. This was purchased in Flanders (at the time annexed by Spain) by Cristóbal García de Castillo, who had been one of the military leaders instrumental in subjugating the Guanches in Gran Canaria. He presented the carving to the church, and apparently it had to be divided into two sections, which were brought to Gran Canaria from Flanders in separate ships. The carved panels depict Nativity scenes.

San Francisco Quarter

Of greatest appeal to most tourists visiting Telde is its San Francisco Quarter. This is best approached from Calle Carlos E Navarro, a picturesque street running off the town's principal thoroughfare. White-washed houses, exposed stonework around doors and windows, and pitched roofs evoke an ancient village. Inspite of the numerous cars that are strangely allowed to park in the cobbled, winding roads, a sense of peace and calm prevails, particularly around the **convent and church of San Francisco**. The latter now serves as a venue for exhibitions and concerts, entry being dependant on the event staged. Although no fittings of interest are to be seen, the coffered ceiling may still be admired.

Additional Information

Acaymo Restaurant
Carretera de Mogán,
Valle de Mogán
☎ 928 569263
Open: 12 noon-10pm
(not Mondays).

Mundo Aborigen
Carretera de Fataga
Open: daily 10am-6pm.

Palmitos Park
Barranco de Chamoriscán
Open: daily 9am-6pm.

Sioux City
Cañón del Aguila
Open: Tuesday to
Sunday 10am-8pm.
Barbecue/dinner
Fridays at 8pm.

N o visitor to the island should neglect to spend some time in Las Palmas, the largest and most important city in the archipelago.

Those arriving in Gran Canaria with no accommodation booked will be able to decide at the very last moment whether or not to head immediately for the city, rather than the southern resorts, as they will have had an up-to-date view of the weather just prior to landing at Gando airport. Bus 60 runs from the airport to Las Palmas, 22km (14 miles) distant, every 30 minutes throughout most of the day. Day-trippers to Las Palmas from the southern resorts are provided with several bus services, but the 30, which runs every 20 minutes, is

direct and by far the quickest. The others, including the 05 night bus, stop everywhere. Note that at the time of writing the last 30 leaves Las Palmas from the Estación de Guaguas in Parque de San Telmo at 9.20pm.

Although a street plan of Las Palmas gives the impression that the city is formidably extensive, for tourists it is really quite small, as only four, easily-managed sections, each of which borders the sea, will be of much interest to them. The most appealing sector architecturally is undoubtedly the old part of the city, formed by the adjacent **Triana** and **Vegueta** quarters. Second in importance is the **Las Canteras Beach** area, where most visitors stay. A brief, uninteresting stretch between Parque de Santa Catalina, just south of Las Canteras, leads to the city's great shopping thoroughfare, **Avenida José Mesa y Lopez**, along which the large stores are grouped. Bisecting the long stretch between the old city and the great shops is **Parque Doramas**, which those with sufficient time available may like to visit, as it in-corporates the Museo de Néstor in the Pueblo Canario and the Hotel de Santa Catalina, the oldest-established luxury hotel in the city.

Accommodation near Las Canteras Beach

Holidaymakers seeking hotels in Las Palmas generally prefer to stay near the magnificent Las Canteras beach. To reach them, municipal buses (guaguas) 1 or 12 to Parque Santa Catalina or Puerto should be taken. Both leave from Avenida Rafael Cabrera (but at different stops), directly outside the bus station (Estación de Guaguas), or from behind Teatro Pérez Galdós in Triana – ask the driver to halt as near as possible to the street required. If seeking budget accommodation, the best area to make for is the north end of Las Canteras, in the side streets of which clean and comfortable *hostals* and *pensiones* may be found. The Mercado de Puerto bus stop is more convenient for this area.

For day visitors from the south wishing to see the most picturesque sector of Las Palmas, the Parque de San Telmo, which faces the bus station, is conveniently located to begin a tour on foot.

The majority of motorists that have hired a car for their entire holiday will understandably drive to Las Palmas, but, as in most of the world's large cities, parking can be difficult and, once the car has been parked, it will prove much easier to tour the old quarter on foot, returning to the vehicle later, perhaps for the half-hour drive to Las Canteras.

As Las Palmas is approached, the truncated tower of the recently restored 16th century **Castillo de San Cristóbal** is passed, overlooking the sea on the right-hand side. At the point where the motorway crosses the Guiniguada ravine there are excellent views, to the left, of the ancient Vegueta quarter of the city, dominated by its great cathedral.

Plaza de España marks the beginning of the great stores of Avenida José Mesa y López

TRIANA QUARTER

T he Triana quarter of Las Palmas gained its name in the early sixteenth century, when many Spaniards emigrated to it from the Triana sector of Seville. It was here that English and Scots first settled early in the nineteenth century, when the British began to establish trading companies in Las Palmas.

Parque de San Telmo

Parque de San Telmo marks the northern border of Triana. In the south-west corner of the park, the small **Ermita de San Telmo**, built in the fifteenth century as a hermitage, is the second oldest church in Gran Canaria.

At no 109, on the west side of the Parque de San Telmo, stands the imposing **Jefatura de Tropas Cuartel General**, the Canary Island's headquarters of the Spanish army, from where Franco proclaimed his opposition to the Republican government on 18 July 1936, thereby setting in motion the Spanish Civil War: a wall plaque commemorates the occasion.

Calle Mayor de Triana

Calle Mayor de Triana, now pedestrianised and paved with granite, is the most important shopping street in the old city. Those staying in Gran Canaria over the Christmas period will be able to admire its renowned decorations. Would-be purchasers should bear in mind that virtually all the shopkeepers are enthusiastic followers of the siesta, and few remain open between 1-4pm. If afternoon shopping is planned, it will be necessary to visit Avenida José Mesa y López in the Alcaravaneras quarter (see page 77), where all the shops, including the city's main department stores, remain open.

On the east side, nos 76 to 86 form a particularly attractive group of Modernist houses, built in the first decade of the 20th century and incorporating colourful ceramic tiles. Calle Torres, fourth right after returning from Calle Perdomo to Calle Mayor de Triana, leads to Calle Cano, first left. On the left, at number 6, is Casa-Museo Pérez Galdós.

Gleaming ceramic tiles on the café in Parque de San Telmo, designed in Spanish Modernist style in 1923

Casa-Museo Pérez Galdós

Here was born, on 10 May 1843, the Canary Islands' most famous novelist, Benito Pérez Galdós. The writer, who like his English contemporary Charles Dickens, exposed social injustices, spent much of his life in Madrid and Santander, and furniture from his properties there is exhibited, including the bed in which he died, on 18 January 1920. Of particular interest is the dining room suite, embellished with ceramics, which was designed by Galdós himself for his house in Madrid.

Although, naturally, the museum has the greatest appeal to Spaniards, entrance is free and provides an opportunity for all to view the interior of a typical nineteenth-century Las Palmas town house, together with its furnishings.

Plaza de Cairasco

From Calle Cano a right then a left turn leads to Calle Peregrina where, at number 1 Patio Peregrina is one of the most popular al fresco cafés in Triana. At the south end of the street, a right turn at Calle Remedios leads to the small but charming Plaza de Cairasco, the name of which commemorates a nineteenth-century Canary poet.

On the north side of this square is another Modernist building, the mid-19th century **Gabinete Literario**, clad with ceramics. Modern works of art by Canarios are frequently on view within this 'literary library'.

On the east side of the square, still identified by a small plaque, is the former Hotel Madrid, where Franco was residing at the outbreak of the Civil War, on 17 July 1936.

Modernist architecture above the shop fronts in Calle Mayor de Triana

South Triana

Calle General Bravo, to the west, separates the plaza from La Alameda a small park originally encircled by railings. In 1892, the 400th anniversary of Christopher Columbus's voyage of discovery to the New World, a commemorative bust of the explorer was erected on a plinth at the north end of the park. Since then, this popular green space, rare in the old quarter of the city, has been known as **Plaza de Colón**.

Occupying the north end of the plaza is the great façade of **San Francisco**, a convent church built in the fifteenth century. Roads southward lead to the Barranco de Guiniguada, which has been partly filled to accommodate a dual carriageway, Carretera Tafira, but was formerly a deep ravine (as it still is further inland), crossed by several bridges.

Remaining on the Triana side, an attractive promenade may be followed seaward towards the **Avenida Marítima del Sur**, which performs a serpentine, multi-level split, prohibiting any maritime views. At the lower end of the promenade, commemorating the site of Puente Palo, the 'commercial' bridge across the Barranco Guiniguada that formerly linked Triana and Vegueta, a delightful, ceramic-faced box screens a duct. On this is reproduced a pictorial map of the ancient area around the bridge. Ahead lies Plaza Stagno, marking the south-east corner of Triana. In its centre stands the Teatro Pérez Galdós.

Teatro Pérez Galdós

This theatre, built in Modernist style in 1919, was named to commemorate the novelist, whose house has been described. Its 'season' is the winter, when concerts, opera and ballet are performed. Most of the theatre's decoration is the work of the renowned Canary painter and sculptor Néstor Martín Fernández de la Torre (1887-1938), who worked primarily in Madrid and Paris, but was always influenced by Canary traditions. It is usually possible to view the great foyer, where the decorative theme (including the carved balustrades) is Canary flora.

The **Teatro Pérez Galdós** is the starting point (Teatro) for many Las Palmas bus routes, which depart from its seaward side. Just west of the theatre's façade, the dual carriageway that now occupies the Barranco Guiniguada may be crossed with safety to Vegueta.

VEGUETA QUARTER

The Vegueta quarter is where Las Palmas was founded in the fifteenth century, and where most of the city's ancient buildings are located. Vegueta means a small area of flat land, and in extent it is little more than a village, albeit a very grand village.

It is known that the slopes of the Barranco Guiniguada were formerly studded with palm trees, and this is how Las Palmas gained its name: none of the trees have survived, nor has any trace of the sixteenth-century wall that once protected the Vegueta and Triana quarters to the north and south.

Mercado Municipal

The Mercado Municipal of Vegueta is the city's longest established and most important market. By tradition, the forty stalls originally led to its being known, cynically, as 'the Market of the Forty Thieves'. Notwithstanding, the prices are now very reasonable, and this is a good place in which to buy charcuterie, cheese and fruit for a picnic lunch. Those unable to visit the small town of Guía, in the north of the island, may wish to buy some *queso de Guía*, a cheese that is unusually flavoured with wild flowers, a Canary speciality. Set in the sides of the market building are a multitude of tiny, economically-

priced bars. Outside the market, small groups of men may be seen discussing the merits of the canaries that are offered for sale in small cages.

At 5-7 Calle Mendizábal, which skirts the market, a Las Palmas institution, El Herreño, specialises in Canarian dishes served either at the restaurant's large bar or in the dining room. Hierro is the least-visited of all the Canary Islands, but it appears to have a tradition of good food, as many of the restaurants in Las Palmas, like this one, are owned by Herreños. Cheese and cheesecake from the island of Hierro is a speciality, and both can be found here.

Calle Mendizábal continues southward to Calle Roque Morera. This street, together with its continuation, **Calle de los Balcones**, is one of the most picturesque in Gran Canaria. At its west end, closing the vista, is the rear of the cathedral.

The eighteenth-century **Centro Atlantico de Arte Moderno** (CAAM), half way up the street at numbers 9-11 houses frequently changing exhibitions.

Running southward from Calle Roque Morera, Calle San Agustín leads to the small **church of San Agustín**, with its bell tower. Adjacent, overlooking the sea, is the **Palacio de Justicia**, which accommodates Gran Canaria's Law Courts.

Return to Calle Mendizábal and turn first left, following Calle Montes de Oca. At number 10, Restaurante Montesdeoca is the prettiest eating place in Las Palmas. It was opened in 1990 in a grand colonial house built in 1515; many will wish to dine al fresco in its cool, galleried patio, fish being the speciality.

Just past the restaurant, where the road opens out to form a plaza, stands the small church or hermitage (Ermita) of **San Antonio Abad**. This was the first church founded in Las Palmas, but the present structure dates from the complete rebuilding of 1892, another Las Palmas commemoration of the discovery of America. It is believed that Christopher Columbus would have heard Mass in the original church on Sunday 26 August 1492, as recorded on the plaque. An extraordinary display of bougainvillaea embellishes the exterior of the building – a delight for photographers. Within, the decor is nineteenth-century baroque.

Casa Museo de Colón
(Columbus Museum)

Streets around the church are narrow and short, but clearly identified. The cobbled **Pasaje Pedro de Algaba** runs southward from **Plaza de San Antonio Abad**, curving around the most famous secular building in the Canary Islands, the Casa-Museo de Colón. (Note that the entrance is at the side of the building, not the door facing the rear of the cathedral.)

The two-storey complex of buildings making up the museum rambles around galleried patios, its chief architectural features being carved doorways, arches and window surrounds in the Isabelline style. Unique to Spain, the name of the style commemorates Queen Isabel (Isabella) I, with whom it is contemporary; its most distinctive feature is profuse sculptural detail applied to Gothic forms, similar in spirit to the almost contemporary Tudor Renaissance work in England.

Following the building's conversion to a museum, items were assembled here from all the Canaries appertaining to the early history of the islands. The main patio is four-sided, and accommodates canons, an eighteenth-century wine vat and an Italian marble font from San Antonio Abad. Painted on the patio's walls are the routes followed by Columbus to the Canary Islands during his first, second and fourth voyages to America.

Linked with the main patio is the three-sided Patio de Armas (Arms), so-named because the ceremony of the governor's guard presenting arms took place here. The central well is contemporary with it. From a third patio, steps ascend to the upper galleries.

Furniture, engravings and paintings are displayed throughout the museum. Included are replicas of *Santa María*, *La Pinta* and *La Niña*, the three caravels that represented the small fleet of Columbus on his first voyage to America; wall maps

Casa Museo de Colón

This late fifteenth-century house was probably built specifically for the island's first Spanish governor, Pedro de Vera, who was certainly residing here in 1482. In the logbook of his flagship *Santa María*, Christopher Columbus records that he landed at Las Palmas on 25 August 1492 for minor repairs to be made to his other two caravels. He stayed until 1 September and, due to the royal patronage he had obtained, it is assumed that the explorer would have been accommodated in the governor's residence. However, as was common with many important events concerning Columbus, this is conjecture. During his second and fourth voyages to America, in 1493 and 1502 respectively, Columbus also stayed for brief periods on the island.

trace the explorer's four expeditions to the New World.

A model of the Castillo de la Luz in its original form shows that it was formerly surrounded by water. In the museum there is a crypt, not always open, with a timber ceiling in which the tombstone of a Guanche princess is displayed.

Another splendid mansion, the **Casa de los Hidalgos**, a nobleman's nineteenth-century residence, adjoins the Casa de Colón.

On leaving the museum, a left turn leads to the rear of the cathedral, overlooking Plaza del Pilar Nuevo. To the south, this plaza has swallowed up all of Calle Francisco María de León and part of Calle Felipe Massieu Falcon, the names of which can still be seen displayed on walls. It seems likely that houses in these streets formerly clustered around the cathedral in a medieval European manner before being cleared for the plaza.

Catedral de Santa Ana & Museo de Arte Sacro

Continue to 20 Calle Espiritu Santo, which skirts the south side of the cathedral, and provides entry to it via the **Museo de Arte Sacro** (Museum of Sacred Art). The cathedral may only be entered free of charge (from its west front) by those attending Mass, and no tours of the building are then permitted.

Many of the exhibits in the Museum of Sacred Art are early American work, some executed by Aztec converts to Christianity. Pre-eminent is an enamelled gold monstrance, attributed to Benvenuto Cellini. Unfortunately, the cathedral's most treasured possession, the fifteenth-century Pendón de la Conquista (Banner of the Conquest), traditionally embroidered personally by Queen Isabella I, is too valuable for permanent display, and may be seen only on special occasions.

Entered from the museum is the Capilla de los Dolores, in the south-east corner of the cathedral. Displayed here, within a glass coffin, is the well-preserved body of the revered Bishop (Obispo) Codina, of the Canaries, who died in 1857; one wonders if this was a conscious revival of the mummifications once practised by the Guanches.

The **cathedral of Santa Ana** was founded in 1497, but not completed in its present form until 1915. Internally, the building is late Gothic with Renaissance elements, while the west façade (seen later) owes its baroque appearance primarily to the eighteenth century. A nave and its flanking north and south aisles, all of the same height, give the appearance of a triple-naved interior. Small windows allow very little natural light, and the cathedral is undoubtedly gloomy.

A statue of the Virgin, by José Luján Pérez, one of the Canario's most important works, is displayed at the north end of the sanctuary.

As usual, the west front was the last major part of the cathedral to be constructed. From its appearance, the façade is of eighteenth- or early nineteenth-century design, the exuberant roofline, the balustrades and the pepperpot cupolas of the twin towers being typically baroque features.

Facing the cathedral are two pairs of bronze dogs, a reference to the huge wild dogs recorded on the islands in early times. It is not known what they looked like, and each of the four depict different breeds – the sculptor hoping, perhaps, that by the law of averages one would be approximately accurate. All possess

Above: Catedral de Santa Ana

Left: One of the bronze dogs facing the cathedral

noble expressions, and Landseer might well have been proud to have cast them. The Canary Islands owe their name to these extinct dogs (*canis* being Latin for dogs) and they have been represented in the coat of arms of the islands since 1506.

Plaza de Santa Ana

After leaving the cathedral and its museum, continue westward along Calle Espiritu Santo to Plaza de Santa Ana, the most important square in Las Palmas. In spite of its classical appearance, the dimensions of the plaza and the functions of the buildings around it have altered little in almost 500 years. It is here that celebrations of major events still take place. At Corpus Christi the paving of the Plaza de Santa Ana is decorated with flowers, laid out in formal patterns.

On the north side of the plaza is the **Palacio Episcopal**, the seat of the bishops of the Canary Islands for many centuries. Although its patio is not open, glimpses may be obtained of the pine door surrounds and balconies typical of the early buildings of the Vegueta.

The **Ayuntamiento** (City Hall) faces the cathedral from the west end of the plaza. It has been here since the sixteenth century, but the present building is mid-nineteenth-century work.

Known as **Casa Regental** (Regent's House), the building on the south side of the plaza was formerly the headquarters of the Spanish forces that guarded the islands. The Inquisition was established in the square in the sixteenth century.

Plaza Espiritu Santo opens out to the south of the Ayuntamiento, its tiny hermitage church having stood for many centuries on the corner with Calle Espiritu Santo.

Museo Canario

Established in the nine teenth century, exhibits in the Museo Canario include geology, pre-history and history; there is also an extensive library and a map collection. Those who have visited Mundo Aborigen, in the south of the island, will be particularly fascinated by exhibits relating to the Guanches, which form the bulk of the collection.

In addition to skeletons and skulls, some of which indicate violent deaths, there are, on the upper floor, a large number of mummies in varying states of preservation, wrapped in goat hides. Guanche utensils, figurines and ceramics demonstrate the artistic abilities of the native people.

Contemporary topographical illustrations of Canary Island towns in the late sixteenth century are an invaluable and fascinating record. Equally invaluable are the library's copies of newspapers published in the Canaries since the late eighteenth century.

Calle Doctor Chil

From the south-west corner of Plaza Espiritu Santo, Calle Luis Millares runs southward to join **Plaza Santo Domingo**, overlooked by its monastic church of the same name. A return northward ends at Calle Doctor Chil, with the **Museo Canario** (see box right) at number 25.

Further down Calle Doctor Chil, at number 17, is the **Seminario Concilia**, founded here in 1777. A plaque records that this was the Ancient College of Jesuits, presented by Carlos III. Its courtyard was restored in 1993. The Jesuit church of the college is typically baroque, its doorway flanked by twisted 'barleysugar' columns.

All the streets leading northward from Calle Doctor Chil return to the dual carriageway separating Vegueta from Triana. From the seaward side of Teatro Pérez Galdós, several buses commence their journeys northward. Most visitors will now wish to continue to Parque de Santa Catalina, a short distance from Las Canteras Beach. Those who prefer to visit Parque Dorama first, followed by the department stores in Avenida José Mesa y López, may conveniently stop off on route.

SANTA CATALINA QUARTER

Las Canteras Beach

Parque de Santa Catalina is undoubtedly the most popular Las Palmas venue for al fresco café life. In recent years, its fashionable status became somewhat diminished by the drop-outs, alcoholics, drug addicts, vagrants and prostitutes who had taken to congregating on its benches, but strenuous efforts have been made to overcome this problem, aided by a costly improvement scheme. The main road, which formerly bisected the park, has been sunk below it, and the buildings on the waterfront side refurbished and converted to cultural purposes. Throughout this turmoil, the city's **Tourist Information Office** (Casa de Turismo), in its Canary-style building, remained open. Jet-foil ferries linking Gran Canaria with the other Canary Islands dock beside the park, and passengers are now presented with a much more attractive introduction to the city than before.

Most buildings on the west side of the park accommodate a bar on the ground floor, with its associated restaurant separated by a public walkway. The dining areas are open to the sky, but may be covered rapidly if the weather turns showery. Menus appear to be similar, concentrating on international dishes as might be expected. Towards the centre, the Rio bar is favoured by the gay community.

Located in the north-east corner, at 6 Calle de Luis Morote, is the **British Consulate**, which will help British holidaymakers in an emer-

gency. Behind the park, the buildings are divided between the red-light district operators and shops selling a bewildering range of cameras, watches and audio equipment: the prices first quoted (both by the importuning girls and the shop assistants) are rarely those eventually paid. Worth visiting, particularly by cigar smokers, is Tabaquería Bazar Marquez, in Calle Ripoche, which runs westward from the centre of the park. Here can be found the finest Palmitos, acclaimed cigars from the nearby island of La Palma.

Playa de Las Canteras
(Las Canteras Beach)
– Northern Section

Calle General Vives runs directly behind the cafés of Parque de Santa Catalina, interconnecting at its east end with **Calle de Sagasta**, which continues northward. After four blocks have been passed, **Paseo de las Canteras** is reached presenting the visitor with a heart-stopping sight – Las Canteras Beach.

Calle de Sagasta runs parallel with Paseo de Las Canteras, adjoining it for several blocks, but most will wish to ascend immediately to the slightly raised promenade. This is the northern end of Playa de Las Canteras, the liveliest sector of the beach, and from where the finest views are obtained. Only here are the local fishermen permitted to beach their boats, and the more mature local residents seem to favour this stretch, laying out their towels and sunbeds between the vessels, thus gaining added protection from any passing breezes, most of which blow down the approach roads to the beach rather than from the sea. At this point, the promenade does an abrupt left turn before finally petering out

Las Canteras Beach

Few of the world's great cities possess a beach at all, let alone a natural beach of golden sand, protected by an off-shore barrier of rocks and almost enclosed by romantic, verdant mountains. It seems strange, therefore, that the internationally renowned Playa de Las Canteras is not more appreciated by tourists to the island – indeed, many of them leave Gran Canaria completely ignorant of its existence.

Nowhere else in the Canary Islands is there a beach that is remotely comparable. Set in a great horseshoe bay open to the west, the open sea is hidden from much of Las Canteras, suggesting that the beach fringes a lake rather than the Atlantic Ocean. Due to the intervening mountains, Las Canteras, unlike the Costa Canaria resorts, suffers little from strong winds, and the water is often significantly warmer because, at low tide, the protective reef creates what is virtually a shallow lagoon. This reef, *La Barra*, is composed of a rare type of rock, known as *canteras*, which has given the beach its name. In a poll taken recently, Las Canteras was voted among the ten most beautiful beaches in the world. Since then, its promenade, Paseo de las Canteras, has been completely remodelled (with the help of EU grants), significantly improving its amenities.

Why then can much of this great beach be relatively deserted when the outstretched bodies of sunbathing holidaymakers leave barely a grain of sand visible at the southern resorts? The answer, of course, is the difference in sunshine hours, which is caused by the moist air carried by the prevailing north-east trade winds rising as the mountains are reached and forming clouds. Nevertheless, when the air pressure is high ,or the wind is in the south-east, Las Canteras can be blessed with days on end of cloudless blue skies; the problem is that such periods cannot be accurately predicted, even though locals recommend March, September and October for the best weather.

into a short headland, known as La Puntilla (the Little Point).

Just off Las Canteras Beach, in side streets such as **Calle La Naval**, low-cost *hostal* accommodation and *pensiones* with private shower and toilet, can still be found. However, if any sleep during the night is anticipated, insist on a rear room overlooking the lightwell of the building. Practically every street in this quarter is packed with bars and discos which, until the early hours of the morning, emit music at full blast, as much to lure in passers-by as to entertain their customers.

La Isleta

Streets running north from Calle La Naval lead to La Isleta, the port workers' area. It is said that long ago this was indeed a small island (*isleta*) before the sand bar built up sufficiently to form an isthmus linking it with the rest of Gran Canaria. Unfortunately, the enticing heights of La Isleta, with their apparently unmatched views of the city, can no longer be approached, as they have been taken over by the military. Columbus landed at La Isleta during an early stage of his second voyage to America, in 1493.

As may be expected, La Isleta is well supplied with *tapas* bars, but tourists are recommended to be careful at night, as muggings have been reported in the quieter streets. Nevertheless, no-one should miss the opportunity of following **Calle de Luján Pérez**, the second street northward from Calle La Naval to Bar Jamón (not Sunday evening or Monday, when it shuts), famous for the high quality of its hams, which are suspended in mainland-Spain fashion from the ceiling. Wine selection is limited but at give-away prices.

A return southward ends at **Calle de Juan Rejón**, and a left turn leads to Castillo de la Luz, set in its small park overlooking **Muelle Pesquero**, the fishing jetty.

Castillo de La Luz

This castle is the city's most ancient and picturesque foundations. An external plaque explains that the present fortress is seventeenth-century work, but this only refers to extensions made to the earlier tower of 1494, which is why a medieval appearance still prevails. The fort, the first to be built by the Spanish in the archipelago, occupies a strategic position, its main purpose being, to deter pirates. For much of its history it was the only defensive tower protecting the approaches to the then tiny settlement of Las Palmas, which lay well to the south.. A succession of naval battles was fought by the Spanish in the harbour of Las Palmas throughout the second half of the sixteenth century, all potential invaders, including Sir Francis Drake, being successfully repulsed.

Complete restoration of the structure took place in the late 1970s, and the castle now accommodates a theatre school. To the north stretches the great port of Las Palmas.

Puerto de la Luz
(Port of Light)

Where Puerto de la Luz has since been excavated there were formerly long beaches of sand. On one of these, the Spanish Conquistadores landed in 1478, as also, so it is believed, did Columbus, 14 years later. Development of Puerto de la Luz was sanctioned

Although partly rebuilt in the seventeenth century, Castillo de la Luz retains its medieval appearance

by the Spanish government in 1881 and, tactfully, a Telde engineer, León y Castillo, brother of Fernando, the Spanish Foreign Minister, was appointed to oversee the huge task: the family name is commemorated by the long thoroughfare that links the old city with the Santa Catalina district. Construction began in 1883, but was not completed until 1902, a tremendous amount of sand being removed. Extensions to the wharves have taken place at regular intervals, and the largest, Muelle Grande, officially renamed Muelle Reina Sofía, is now almost 4km ($2\frac{1}{2}$ miles) long.

Returning in the direction of Las Canteras, the Mercado del Puerto is sited where the coast road bends to the left. Basically a food market, it was entirely reconstructed in 1995. The Sunday morning flea market of Las Palmas, El Rastro, has been relocated in recent years from the Vegueta quarter, and is now held in front of the Mercado del Puerto, overlooking the water.

Playa de las Canteras – Southern Section

A succession of short streets lead westward from the Mercado del Puerto to Las Canteras Beach, and most will wish to follow one of them in order to return to the promenade. Relatively few high-rise buildings overlook Las Canteras: most that do are hotels, some of which, after years in the doldrums, have been remodelled and upgraded recently. This is indicative of the areas return to favour with tourists, prompted by the regeneration of the *paseo*. Two very grand hotels overlook the beach, both five-star graded: Meliá las Palmas and Reina Isabel. Between them runs what is by far the most architecturally attractive stretch of the *paseo*, a mix of traditional Canary-style houses with pine balconies, and examples of Spanish Modernism – villas built in the 1920s on virgin sand.

Once these have been past most eyes will be cast perpetually seaward to the undulating mountains and, at last, as the bay widens out, to the open sea. On reasonably clear days, Tenerife's great Mount Teide can be seen dominating the horizon, but to its left is another, but much nearer, extinct volcanic cone, with which it is sometimes confused. This is Montaña de Gáldar, which can be visited during an excursion to Gran Canaria's north coast (see page 83).

It is the changing light and cloud formations, as much as the golden

The marina

sand and scenery, that make Las Canteras so special – even on cloudy days. In the morning, when the sun catches the mountains, the modelling is pronounced, and they appear to be quite close. Conversely, in the evening, with the setting sun behind them, they form a mysterious black silhouette, seemingly far distant.

Calle Olof Palmer leads inland from the promenade to **Avenida José Mesa y López** and **Plaza de España** (formerly Plaza de la Victoria), a popular late-evening assembly point for the city's youngsters, who frequent its outdoor cafés (see photo page 60).

THE ALCARAVANERAS QUARTER & THE GREAT STORES

Avenida José Mesa y López, **which runs through Plaza de España, is the most important shopping street in modern Las Palmas – chic boutiques vying with large department stores for the shopper's attention.**

Before continuing further seaward, follow **Calle Galicia**, first right, to the Mercado Central of Las Palmas, where the usual lively stalls drastically undercut the prices demanded in the food halls of El Corte Inglés, just three blocks away. Overlooking the southern end of the market, at 5 **Calle de Barcelona**, is La Habana, open daily from 5am, and where the city's favourite *churros con chocolate* is served: the chocolate is so rich and thick that a spoon almost stands up in it.

Calle Valencia runs southward from the east side of the market and, seven blocks away, on its corner with **Calle Manuel González Martín** (number 36), Hermanos Rogelio, a popular bar/restaurant, serves genuine Canarian dishes Monday to Saturday at reasonable prices. Eat at the bar or at a table; there is always a lively atmosphere, which can become frenetic on big match days at the nearby football stadium, **Estadio Insular**.

On the northern side of the market, but not part of it, La Garriga, in **Calle Néstor de la Torre**, is renowned for its *charcuterie*, much of it ready prepared for an al fresco lunch.

Returning to Avenida José Mesa y López, almost directly opposite El Corte Inglés, at number 15, is Galerías Preciados, a branch of the rival department store chain, which is not quite so up-market as El Corte Inglés. Few will be able to resist the welcoming entrance, at number 18, Avenida José Mesa y López, of the largest store in the Canaries, El Corte Inglés (see box below).

At the end of the busy avenue is a jetty with, at its southern end, the Club Náutico. This overlooks the golden sands of **Playa de las Alcaravaneras**, once generally popular but, since the busy Avenida Marítima del Norte was laid out directly behind it, the beach has become the haunt, almost exclusively, of local youngsters.

El Corte Inglés

El Corte Inglés is a member of the chain of department stores now represented in most large Spanish cities, which has gained an international reputation. The quality of goods sold matches that of London's Selfridges, although the food halls are even more extensive. The name El Corte Inglés (The English Cut) surprises many. It has been inherited from the original tailor's shop in Madrid, where both the cloth imported and the styles adopted were English. Don Ramón Areces borrowed £800 to buy the shop in 1934; it prospered, enabling him to build a department store empire with a turnover now exceeding £3 billion. Cash was paid for each new store as it was built, and the group remained in private hands. When Areces died in 1989 he was believed to be the wealthiest man in Europe.

Although prices are not cheap, the quality is guaranteed, any faulty goods being replaced without question. Of particular interest to holidaymakers will be the wines and spirits and food halls. In the latter will be found high quality *charcuterie* and cheeses from all over Spain – not just the Canary Islands. Look for the blue-veined goats milk cheese, *Cabrales*, from Asturias, not easily found elsewhere in Gran Canaria.

THE CIUDAD JARDÍN QUARTER

Constructed in the 1930s, between the Alcaravaneras district and the commercial quarter of Lugo, Ciudad Jardín (Garden City) was inspired by English examples of the period, but with houses designed in a modern rationalist, rather than a traditional style.

The area is pleasant, although lacking exceptional interest for tourists; its most attractive sector is sandwiched between **Calle Pio XII** and **Calle León y Castillo**, in the centre of which stands the **English Church**, entered from **Calle Brasil**. Walkers must be prepared to make several east or west deviations in order to maintain a southerly route towards Parque Dorama, as thoroughfares tend to be short and rarely interconnect directly ahead. Most, however, will prefer to take bus number 1 from Avenida José Mesa y López direct to Parque Dorama. Facing the park, the new bars/restaurants built around the jetty have become fashionable in the evenings.

Parque Dorama

Parque Dorama, the jewel of the Ciudad Jardín development, is the largest park in Las Palmas, and provides a green break immediately before the rather grey commercial quarter of Lugo is reached. To the right of its entrance is Hespeira, long regarded as the best florists in Las Palmas.

In the south-west corner of the park, the **Santa Catalina Hotel** welcomes visitors to its bars, garden and restaurants. Opened in 1884, this five-star hotel has been luxuriously refurbished, and is still the most prestigious in Las Palmas the old-world atmosphere being unmatched elsewhere in the Canaries. Originally designed by McLauren, a Scottish architect, the hotel was also built by a British contractor. The Santa Catalina incorporates a casino, where smart (but not formal) dress and a passport are required. The Doramas restaurant is regarded by

Pueblo Canario & Museo Néstor

Pueblo Canario (Canary Village) was designed by the painter Néstor de la Torre, who died suddenly in 1938, before it was finished. His brother Miguel, an architect, completed the building work, and then remodelled and extended the Santa Catalina Hotel. On Thursday evenings and Sunday mornings, Canary folk-dancing is performed in the Pueblo's courtyard, a rare opportunity for photographers, as traditional costumes are now seldom worn elsewhere on the island.

The **Museo Néstor** is to be found on the south side of the courtyard. Many of the artist's possessions are displayed, as also are his designs for several buildings in the *pueblo*, two of which were built, and a *parador* at Cruz de Tejeda, which was not. The most important of Néstor's works, however, are his set of eight paintings, *Poema de la Mer* (Poem of the Sea), displayed in a circular, domed gallery.

many as the city's finest. *Tartana*, horsedrawn carriages may be hired outside the hotel for city tours.

South of the hotel is the Pueblo Canario, incorporating the Museo Nestor (see box opposite).

In the south-west corner of the park is a small **zoo**, and in the north-west corner, the **Julio Navarro open-air swimming pool**, only used in summer. Although the park ends at **Calle Emilio Ley**, gardens are laid out ahead, and reach up to the heights of Altavista. This quarter begins on the west side of **Paseo del Chil**, where there is a waterfall monument to Fernando León y Castillo.

Bus 3 departs from Triana's **Avenida 1º de Mayo**, linking the western hillside suburbs of Las Palmas before descending, via Avenida José Mesa y López, to Parque de Santa Catalina and the port. For much of the journey, passengers gain splendid birds-eye views of the city.

Additional Information

ACCOMMODATION

Meliá las Palmas Hotel *****
6 Calle Gomera
☎ 928 267600 Fax 928 268411

Santa Catalina Hotel *****
Parque Dorama, ☎ 928 243040

Sandra P **
Calle La Naval 9, ☎ 928 262800

PLACES TO VISIT

Casa Museo de Colón
1 Calle Colón
Open: Monday-Friday 9am-6pm;
Saturday and Sunday 9am-3pm).

**Catedral de Santa
Ana/Museo de Arte Sacro**
20 Calle Espiritu Santo
Open: Monday-Friday 10am-5pm;
Saturday 9am-2pm.

Casa-Museo Pérez Galdós
6 Calle Cano
Open: Monday-Friday 9am-1pm.

Museo Canario
25 Calle Dr Chil
Open: Monday-Friday 10am-5pm;
Saturday and Sunday 10am-2pm.

Pueblo Canario & Museo Néstor
Parque Dorama
Open: Tuesday-Friday 10am-1pm
and 4pm-8pm; Sunday 11am-2pm.

TOURIST INFORMATION OFFICES

Parque de Santa Catalina
☎/Fax 928 264623
Open: Monday-Friday 9am-2pm.

17 Léon y castilla
☎ 928 362222

Parque de Santa Catalina
Open: Monday-Friday 9am-2pm
☎ 928 264623 Fax 928 229820

Gando Airport
☎ 928 574058 or 928 574044

5 Itineraries from Las Palmas

The northern itineraries described begin at Las Palmas, but motorists driving from the south who possess a good road map (and a degree of extra-sensory perception) will be able, in some cases, to avoid the city centre. Drivers should be aware that if they approach the city from the south and wish to take the 811 to Vega de San Mateo or the 813/817 to Teror then they **must not** miss the turn offs. Apart from an exit to the suburb of San José to the south of the city centre, these are the only two ways of leaving the *Autopista*, and if missed motorists will end up at the port or on the north coast. Those relying on bus services, must remember that all journeys in the north begin and end at the Estación de Guagas in Las Palmas. All the excursions already described from the south can also, of course, be started at Las Palmas. Those travelling by bus between Las Palmas and the south-west coast resorts or San Augustín should ensure that they take the 31, which departs every 30 minutes from Puerto Rico following the *carretera* and bypassing Playa del Inglés, with its many stops, thereby reducing the journey time significantly.

THE NORTH COAST

Gran Canaria's north coast, well-watered and fertile, was a popular residential area of the Guanches, and all its existing townships of any size were established long before the Spanish conquest. Its appeal consists of dramatic cliffs and strange-shaped rocks rather than golden sandy beaches. Bear in mind that this coast tends to be affected by cloud that builds up over the central mountains and can turn showery, particularly in the afternoons.

As opposed to the west side of the island, a good road closely follows the north coast, and bus services are frequent, particularly between Las Palmas and Gáldar. The approach to the north coast road from Las Palmas is made via its dreary south-west suburb of Guanarteme; it is sad to reflect that delightful, Maspalomas-style sand dunes at the back of Playa de Las Canteras were removed in the 1950s for its construction.

If staying in the Las Canteras area, particularly at the south end, some may prefer to walk or taxi as far as the bridge that crosses the *barranco* after Guanarteme has been left. Here, the north coast buses halt, thus obviating the slow and lengthy journey to the bus station at Parque San Telmo and back again.

Buses 103 and 105 all follow the same coastal roads to Gáldar; the 101, a very limited service,

Palm trees blend with conifers at surprisingly high levels in the mountains

continues to San Nicolás de Tolentino (see page 45), via Puerto de las Nieves; the 103 links Agaete with the coast at Puerto de las Nieves, and the 102 continues along the valley from Puerto de las Nieves to Los Berrazales. The new Guia/Gáldar bypass has recently opened, primarily to serve the new inter-island ferry services from Agaete; changes to the bus services are expected in consequence.

Bañadero & Puente de Silva

There are fine views of the receding Las Canteras beach and La Isleta from the road as it curves northward. At the small town of **Bañadero**, a left turn branches inland to Arucas and Teror; some may prefer to make the detour at this stage, and it is described on pages 87-8. Bañadero, with a maritime esplanade, is named

from its natural rock pools, in one of which a Guanche princess was captured by Spanish invaders.

Several steep *barrancos* reach the sea after **Pagador** has been passed; two of them are crossed by the **Puente de Silva**, a double-stage viaduct, the highest in Spain, and known locally as the Salto del Canario (Canario's Leap).

It is here that the great banana plantations of the north begin. Unfortunately for the Canarios, cheaper bananas are now obtainable from elsewhere to supply the European market, and the crop is in decline, much of it now unattended and growing wild. This does, however, provide the attractive, but once rare sight of bright yellow bananas hanging from the trees; formerly, all were picked green for slow ripening in the holds of ships and warehouses.

Guía

Guía is a prosperous agricultural town, which now virtually merges with Gáldar. It was the birthplace of the most famous Canarian sculptor, José Luján Pérez (1756-1815), whose work is seen in the cathedral at Las Palmas; further examples are to be found in Guía's **church of Santa María**, founded in 1491. A pilgrimage to the church, known as the Romería de las Marías, is made during the last week in September on a variable date. Traditional costumes are worn and there is much dancing and feasting to end this popular event.

Buses, of course, link Guía with Gáldar, but the distance between the towns is short, and many without cars will opt to walk, particularly as the 810 has lost its dual carriageway status at Guía, and there are attractive views from the road along the Barranco de Gáldar, which opens up to join the lush Agaete valley.

As Gáldar is approached, the 'mini Mount Teide', distantly observed from Playa de Las Canteras, comes into view to the north. Known as the Montaña or Pico de Gáldar, this extinct volcano retains a symmetrical, conical shape, but its stony slopes have led to its being referred to, rather unkindly, as 'the slag heap'.

Gáldar

In addition to being an agricultural town, Gáldar is the commercial centre of Gran Canaria's north west. A market is held every Thursday morning in **Plaza Mayor**, but cheap clothing now dominates, and it is not very exciting.

Gáldar was a regional capital of the Guanches, possibly one of the earliest in Gran Canaria, and artefacts made by them and discovered locally are displayed in a small museum in the town hall; this faces the church from the west side of the plaza, where there grows a venerable dragon tree, of which the locals are rather proud.

Gáldar's church is dedicated to **Santiago** (St James) **de los Caballeros**, as the town fell to the Spanish on 25 July, St James's Feast Day. An early seventeenth-century church, built where the Guanche king's house

Queso de flora

Just outside Guía, at 17 Carretera General Lomo Guillen, on the main road to Gáldar, is the Artesanía Canaria, better known as Arturo's Bar, where the famous local cheese, *queso de flora*, may be eaten or purchased to take away. This cheese is made from goats' milk flavoured with the blossoms of a type of thistle known as cardoon. Arturo serves it with the surprising combination of garlic potatoes and hot toast. A selection of Canary wines, difficult to find elsewhere, may also be tasted: the dry, red Monte Déniz, from the Santa Brígida region, is the best accompaniment to *queso de flora*, but those with a sweet tooth should ask for the white Vino de Licor Dulce, which is probably similar to the Canary malmsey wine, *malvasías*, so popular in Shakespeare's England. Crafts as well as cheeses may be purchased here; particularly attractive are the knives with inlaid bone handles, known as *cachillos*, and *cajas*-decorated boxes, both locally made.

Cueva Pintada

Discovered in the nineteenth century, Gáldar's most famous attraction, the Cueva Pintada, contains the only Guanche wall paintings yet found in the Canaries. Almost square in plan, the cave's 3m (10ft) high walls are decorated with geometric paintings in red, white and black. Experts believe that the work was executed around the time of the birth of Christ, but its significance is a mystery; the apparent rarity of such decoration may indicate that an important Guanche chief inhabited the cave. In 1970, deterioration of the paintings had become apparent and the cave was blocked for thirty years, but it has now reopened in conjunction with a new museum.

and a small Spanish fort once stood, was rebuilt and enlarged in the eighteenth century. Within are sculptures by Pérez, and the *pilar verde* (green font) in which, by tradition, Guanche converts to Christianity were baptised.

Antonio Padrón (1920-68), a Gáldar artist, followed the Impressionist style, and his work is exhibited in the house where he painted, **Casa-Museo de Antonio Padrón**, at 1 Calle Drago, and where, apart from five years studying in Madrid, he spent his entire life.

From the north side of Plaza Mayor, a narrow street leads through banana plantations towards the coast where, approximately 1 mile distant, **La Guancha**, an ancient necropolis, was discovered in 1935. Truncated rock circles, right of the path, are the burial sepulchres of Guanches.

Sardina del Norte

A local bus to and from Sardina follows the second turn right (140) off the main road, once Gáldar has been left, for 6km (4 miles). Many will find the beach and cafés of the small port the most attractive on the north coast, even though the sand is grey. The coastal scenery is magnificent, with particularly good views from **Punta de Sardina**, a headland to the north, which embrace Tenerife in clear weather. Sardina has a small church and, at the end of its sheltered bay, a lighthouse.

Reptilandia Park

Motorists returning towards the 810 will be able to follow a track, right, to Reptilandia Park. Others must take the Gáldar/Agaete bus (101, 102, 103) from the main road, and alight at the Cruz de Pineda stop. A large sign near this indicates the track to Reptilandia Park, which spreads over the lower slopes of another stony, extinct volcano, **Montaña Almago**. The most exotic specimens of reptiles in the collection of over a hundred species are the poisonous snakes and frogs, all of which are kept safely behind glass in the visitors centre. However, the bulk of the reptiles on view are harmless lizards, some of them brightly coloured, which are kept in open enclosures.

Cuevas de las Cruces

A minor road leads eastward from the Cruz de Pineda bus stop to the Cuevas de las Cruces, a short walk away. These caves are still occupied, many of them having been in the possession of the same family for generations, although it is almost certain that the original residents were Guanches. Nearby, the **Ermita de San Isidro el Viejo** is one of the tiniest chapels on the island.

Agaete

Standing at the entrance to the Barranco de Agaete, the most fertile valley in the north of the island, the town's main purpose, as might be expected, is to serve as a distribution centre for agricultural produce. Whitewashed 'cubic' houses give Agaete a very Moorish appearance.

Bajada de la Rama

On 4 August each year Agaete is witness to the only Guanche rite still performed anywhere in the Canaries. Known as Bajada de la Rama (Cutting of the Branch), local residents trek to the Tamadaba pine forest at dawn, returning to Agaete with huge branches that they have cut from the trees – a 6 to 8 hour expedition. The branches are then taken to Puerto de las Nieves, nearby, where the sea is symbolically beaten with them. Originally, the purpose of this superstitious rite was to persuade the autumn rains not to fail, but it is now just an excuse for a *fiesta*, and has long been Christianised. No longer does the rite end at the shore, as, after it has ended, the townsfolk gather in Agaete, singing and dancing in the streets until the early hours of the following morning.

Puerto de las Nieves

The 103 bus links Agaete with **Puerto de las Nieves**, via a minor road, but it is not a long walk.

Many surmise, erroneously, that Nieves (Snows) refers to the gleaming winter snows of Mount Teide, which can usually be seen clearly from here, but it is, in fact, a painting in the **Ermita de las Nieves** chapel that gave the small port its name. This sixteenth-century Flemish triptych, generally regarded as the greatest artistic treasure of Gran Canaria,

A small extinct volcano the Pico de Gáldar overlooks the small town below it

was brought to the island by an Italian, Antón Cerezo, who settled on the island. Due to its subject matter, the work is known as the *Virgen de las Nieves* (Virgin of the Snows). Unfortunately, due to the painting's great value, the recently restored chapel is locked unless Mass is being celebrated; Sunday, therefore, is the best day to make a visit. If the chapel is open, also look out for the model sailing ships on display.

Puerto de las Nieves, primarily a fishing village, possesses two beaches, both of stone and dark sand: foaming breakers often make swimming impossible. To the south, the jagged peaks of the Tamadaba massif provide a dramatic backdrop. A smart new promenade, **Paseo de las Poetas** (Poet's Walk), has made access between the beaches much easier.

Sternly pointing skyward, a slim volcanic rock, known as **Dedo de Dios** (Finger of God), is located at the west end of the beach. From a

distance, the rock can be difficult to identify because, particularly on dull days, it merges into the background of equally black cliffs.

From Puerto de las Nieves, the 102 bus follows the delightful, 7km (4½ miles) long, Barranco de Agaete to its head at **Los Berrazales**.

Bus 102 returns to Las Palmas; those continuing southward by bus to San Nicolás de Tolentino and thence Puerto de Mogán must take the 101. Although nothing exceptional is passed on route to San Nicolás, some invigorating coastal scenery can be glimpsed; passengers should try to find a seat on the right-hand side of the bus.

Motorists returning to Las Palmas may have sufficient time to make a detour to Arucas and Teror by turning right at Bañaderos, following the 813. Bus 215, which starts on the coast at Pagador, also connects these towns, via Bañaderos, Cardones, Tenoya and Tamaraceite.

THE PICTURESQUE NORTHERN TOWNS

Church of San Juan Bautista, Arucas

From Las Palmas, motorists will take the 813 to Arucas; this runs inland and then keeps parallel with the north-coast road; buses 205, 206, 209, 211 and 234 link Las Palmas with Arucas, following various routes.

Arucas

Arucas is still given the accolade as the third largest town in Gran Canaria (after Las Palmas and Telde), even though the conurbation based on Playa del Inglés is now very much more extensive.

Architecturally, Arucas is dominated by its huge church of **San Juan Bautista** (St John the Baptist). Consecrated in 1917, local craftsmen laboured on the Neo-Gothic building for almost a century. A contrast between white-painted plaster and exposed basalt, in the traditional Canary style, enlivens the façade. Within are found works by local artist, Juan de Miranda, a sixteenth-century

Arucas rum

Rum lovers may already have tasted the pale gold liquid in bottles displaying the name Ron Arucas, which will be found in all bars in Gran Canaria. This rum has been made in Arucas virtually ever since sugar cane was introduced to the islands, and is the prime reason why the crop is still grown in the area. The Ron Arehucas (the old spelling of Arucas) distillery is located surprisingly close to the town centre, and visitors are welcomed with a tipple.

Flemish painting of the Nativity and, of greatest importance, a carved figure of Christ, by Manuel Ramos. Also noteworthy is the stained glass, rated the best in Gran Canaria. Locals, with an excess of local pride, often refer to their church, erroneously, as the 'cathedral'.

Also not to be missed in Arucas are the town's subtropical public gardens.

From the town centre, a short minor road climbs northward to the summit of **Montaña de Arucas**, from where the coastal views towards La Isleta are outstanding.

Firgas & Moya

From Arucas, the 814 runs westward to Firgas, a name with which visitors to Gran Canaria soon become familiar, as the eponymous best-selling mineral water on the island is produced from the natural springs which flow south of the village. Moya is reached by making a brief return northward on the 814, followed by a left turn on the 100, and another on the 160. The 211 bus from Arucas follows the same route; buses 116 and 117 link Moya directly with Las Palmas.

Doramas, the last Guanche king, had his military headquarters at Moya, and the town was also the birthplace, at 1 Paseo Tomás Morales, of the poet Tomás Morales (1885-1921), whose house may be visited.

Of greatest interest in Moya is the location of its twin-towered church, **Nuestra Señora de la Candelaria**, perched dramatically on the cliff overlooking the Moya *barranco*. Its position is best appreciated from across the *barranco* on the 150 road to Guía, rather than from the town itself. Earlier churches on this site, dating from the sixteenth century, were apparently unable to survive the exposed situation, wind and rain gradually eroding their structures.

Those following the 814 by car or bus from Firgas to Teror will pass the bottling plant of the mineral water (Aguas de Firgas), which is available in aerated (*gas*) or non-aerated (*sin gas*) form. The road then takes an abrupt turn eastward, descending in sharp bends to Teror, lying serenely in the valley below.

Teror

Holidaymakers in Gran Canaria should make every effort to visit this beautiful town, which bus 216 links directly with Las Palmas. Here will be seen the finest examples on the island of pine balconies, the hallmark of Canary architecture.

Located on the same square as the church is the ancient **Casa de la Villa** (town hall), and its patio may be entered.

The street that directly faces the church is renowned for its balconies. Canary balconies are often canopied and usually face north, emphasising that they are certainly not intended for sunbathing.

Nuestra Señora del Pino

The most picturesque quarter of Teror is centred on its church, Nuestra Señora del Pino. Its name refers to the tradition that, in 1481, the Virgin Mary appeared on the branch of a pine tree to the village priest. The church, founded in 1515 as a simple building without aisles, was gradually extended. In 1718, fireworks for a local *fiesta*, stored in the sacristy, accidentally exploded, causing extensive damage. As rebuilding of the church depended on local finance, it was not until the end of the eighteenth century that the new building was completed. A baroque façade, as usual, combines white paintwork with exposed stone. Separate from the main church is the octagonal bell tower, which is surprisingly designed to imitate the late Gothic, sixteenth-century Manueline style of Portugal.

Within, the ceiling is coffered and there is some fine carving. Set in the reredos of the high altar, an illuminated alabaster Madonna and Child carving, known as the Virgin of the Pines, is sumptuously robed. This was made in 1767, and the throne of solid silver, the work of a Tenerife silversmith, is believed to be contemporary with it. The Blessed Virgin of Teror is the patron saint of Gran Canaria, and there are great celebrations on her Feast Day, 8 September, when pilgrims arrive in decorated carts.

Until the present century, it was a superstitious custom, whenever drought or a locust plague threatened, to march in procession from Teror to Las Palmas cathedral, bearing this figure, which was supplicated to intervene. Even today, the carving is accredited with healing powers.

Teror is noted for its attractive pine balconies

Immediately left of the church is the **Casa Museo Patronas de la Virgen**, a mansion with a galleried patio, which has been in the ownership of the aristocratic Manrique de la Lara family since the seventeenth century, and where its members frequently continue to reside in the summer (Teror is a popular inland summer resort). For the rest of the year, apart from Fridays, the house is open to the public, and the family's collection of furniture and objets d'art may be viewed.

The name of Teror's **Plaza de Bolivar** commemorates the birth in a house overlooking this square of the mother of Simón Bolivar, who gained independence from the Spanish for several colonies in South America, one of which, Bolivia, bears his name.

Every Sunday morning, the market held in the town is particularly noted for local produce. Always available in Teror is nougat (*turrón*) and intricate lacework made by nuns in the nearby convent. A local *charcuterie* store, **Las Nueces**, is noted for the quality of its homemade *chorizo* and black pudding.

Good food can be obtained from **Bar Americano**, facing the church, and **Bar Diego**, in Calle de General Franco, where the *carne de cabra* (goat meat) is delicious. For those requiring a more formal meal, **El Secuestro** offers local specialities and charcoal grilled meat (closed Mondays).

From Teror, the 814 leads directly to Vega de San Mateo, or San Mateo (see page 95) passing close to the extinct volcano of **Pino Santo**, where the miracle of the virgin's appearance is said to have occurred. Here can be seen the only dragon tree growing wild in the north of Gran Canaria.

West of Teror

From Teror westward, the 814 links with the 110, which climbs steadily uphill towards Valleseco and the mountain village of Artenara. Bus 220 from Las Palmas follows the route.

On the left is passed the Balcón de Zamora *mirador*, on the summit of which is a large bar/restaurant specialising in Canary dishes. The road to Artenara passes through the villages of **Valleseco** and **Lanzarote**, the name of the latter, like that of the island of Lanzarote, commemorating Lancellotto Mallocello, the fourteenth-century Genoese navigator, who rediscovered the Canary Islands. Unattractive piles of volcanic rock, known as *malpais* (bad country), are gradually being hidden by the planting of pine trees.

Just after **Cuevas Corcho**, the 110 abruptly turns right and climbs steeply. It should be noted that both the left turn at this point and that which follows lead to the **Cruz de Tejeda** and the high peaks of Gran Canaria (see page 55). On route to Artenara there are tremendous views from **Pinos de Gáldar** to the north coast. The name of this viewpoint reflects that the cone-shaped Montaña de Gáldar can be seen in the distance.

Artenara & Pinar de Tamadaba

Artenara, at 1,219m (3,998ft) above sea level, is the highest village in Gran Canaria. Caves in the region, some still occupied, indicate that the Guanches lived in the area. There is a small church in the village, but of greater interest is the **Santuario de la Virgen de la Cuevita**, the chapel of the patron saint of Artenara. It is reached by a winding road, which begins opposite the church. A cottage industry of replicating Guanche artefacts and red pottery for sale to tourists has evolved in the village. The famous **La Silla** restaurant at Artenara is located partly in a cave, partly on a terrace with superb views. It closes at sunset.

Continuing westward from Artenara, the 3.1 road encircles **Pinar de Tamadaba**, the largest forest of Canary pines on the island, ending abruptly at the entrance to a forestry station. The trees even cover the summit of the **Pico de Tamadaba** (1,444m/4,736ft), which rises from its centre. Within the ICONA picnic site there is a welcome spring-water drinking fountain, and rocky ledges offer Gran Canaria's finest views of Mount Teide emerging from the sea.

The quickest return for motorists to Las Palmas is made via Cruz de Tejeda, following the 811 San Mateo/ Santa Brígida road, a route which is described from the direction of Las Palmas in the next section. Those making for the southern resorts will follow the 811 from Cruz de Tejeda to Ayacata, followed by the 815 to San Bartolomé, and the 12.1, via Fataga, to Playa del Inglés, the route described (in reverse order) on page 55.

THE 'PARADISE' ROUTE TO THE MOUNTAINS

This relatively short excursion begins at the Carretera del Centro (the 811), which divides the Vegueta and Triana quarters of Las Palmas; it then runs above the Barranco de Guiniguada and ends at San Mateo. On Sunday mornings, an important market is held at San Mateo, and in order not to miss it some may wish to proceed directly to this small town. A continuation from San Mateo to the high mountains is easily made.

Numerous buses from Las Palmas, are routed along various stages of the 811. The 00 guagua stops at the entrance to **Jardín Canario** and continues to **Santa Brígida**; the 58 and 59 terminate at **Tafira Alta**; the 301 and 302 terminate at Santa Brígida; the 303 and 305 continue to San Mateo and (the 305 only) to **Tejeda**.

What are undoubtedly the most desirable residential suburbs of Las Palmas spread along the 811, the lush gardens of their houses, always green and blossoming, giving the impression of a large park studded with buildings. The entire area is renowned throughout the Canaries for the high quality of its restaurants, catering not only for wealthy Canarios, but also for the sizeable number of foreign immigrants residing in this part of the island, attracted by its benign climate.

Feathery eucalyptus trees, of Australian origin, line the road, while in the valleys below, spiky palm trees provide an exotic contrast. Depictions of the scenery in paradise are evoked.

Jardín Canario

Lying just north of the 811, this immense garden, officially called the Viera y Clavijo Canary Garden, was founded by Sventenius, a Swede, and opened in 1952. The layout is informal, and a natural appearance has been achieved. As would be expected, most of the specimens are from the Canary Islands, but virtually any plant life that will thrive in Gran Canaria's balmy climate is eligible for inclusion. Particularly impressive are the towering cacti from South Africa.

Overlooking the garden and the surrounding countryside from its cliff-top location is the **Jardín Canario restaurant**, formerly a residential *parador*. Canary specialities and the usual international dishes are on offer (check if credit cards are accepted yet).

The huge crater of the extinct volcano at Bandama

La Calzada

South of Jardín Canario spreads the village of La Calzada, where there are two restaurants worth seeking out: **Grill La Raqueta**, located on the *carretera*, specialising in charcoal grills, and **Los Conejos**, at 18 La Calzada (closed Tuesdays), where the rabbit, Canary-style, is superb.

At the end of the village, a bridge crosses the *barranco*. Two Spanish monks, bent on converting Guanches to Christianity, were murdered in caves that had been excavated in the cliff on the far side; they are now known as **Cuevas de los Frailes** (Caves of the Monks).

Tafira Alta & Monte Coello

A return to the 811 leads to Tafira Alta, possibly the most sought-after (and expensive) of all the residential areas in the north of the island. Only the extremely wealthy can afford to live here. It was developed at the turn of the century by the British, many of whom were making a fortune from their introduction of new crops to the Canaries, particularly bananas. The late-nineteenth-century **Los Frailes Hotel**, built by an Englishman, still functions in the town, on the *carretera*. Tafira Alta merges to the south with **Monte Coello** (or simply El Monte), the most important wine producing town in Gran Canaria.

From Monte Coello, the 13.5 leads eastward to Gran Canaria's most famous extinct volcanic crater, **Caldera Bandama**. Buses 311 or 312 provide a service to Bandama from Las Palmas, following the 811 before turning eastward on the 320 and then the 13.6 to La Atalaya.

La Atalaya

It is said that more than 1,000 Guanche caves exist in and around La Atalaya, many of them still inhabited. Pottery made locally can be purchased in the village.

Caldera Bandama

The 13.6 now winds northward to join the 13.5, spiralling round the slopes of **Pico de Bandama**, which rises 574m (1,883ft) above sea level. The fertile volcanic crater (*caldera*) has a circumference of about 1,000 metres (3,300ft), and a depth of 200m (650ft). Much of it is arable land, and farm buildings below may clearly be seen from the crater's rim.

On the west side of the mountain is Spain's oldest golf course, the **Club de Golf de Las Palmas**, founded by British residents in 1891.

A return to the 811, either at Monte Coello or the 312 junction further south, must be made before continuing to the high mountains. The road climbs ever upward, and the scenery becomes even more idyllic as the dramatic background of peaks is approached. In late January/early February, when the almond trees are in blossom, this part of Gran Canaria is quite breathtaking in its pastoral magnificence – if depicted on a chocolate box it would be considered unacceptably over the top.

Santa Brígida

Santa Brígida must be passed before the ribbon of luxury villas is interrupted by open country, but it will be noted that on both sides of the road buildings struggle heroically to retain a hold on precipitous mountain slopes. Santa Brígida is of no particular interest to tourists, in fact, it is hard to clearly distinguish architecturally between any of the fashionable developments along this mountain road. A famous Santa Brígida restaurant, **La Grutas de Artiles**, is located at Las Meleguinas, and offers beautifully prepared Spanish and international dishes. Two of the dining rooms are set in caves and, in summer, clients may use the private swimming pool.

Mano de Hierro

Lovers of German food should visit Mano de Hierro, founded by German-born Karl Kenegeter, and now run by his son. Knowledgeable German visitors enthuse over the restaurant's home-made sausages and *patés,* which are now almost impossible to obtain made in the traditional style in their own country; the *quesadilla* (cheesecake) is exceptional.

San Mateo
(Vega de San Mateo)

A drop in temperature often becomes apparent at San Mateo, due to its altitude. The small town is still chiefly dependant on agriculture, and retains a slightly more venerable appearance than its neighbours, although, like them, it is also a popular residential centre. On Sunday mornings, a large farmer's market is held, where the prices of the fruit and vegetables are said to be some of the lowest on the island; locally produced white cheese, *queso San Mateo*, is naturally found at its best here. Anyone wishing to purchase a goat will also find a bargain!

Virtually all holidaymakers who approach the high mountains from Las Palmas will take the route just described, as the Carretera del Centro is by far the easiest and fastest way of reaching them. Many, therefore, will continue ahead from San Mateo to the high mountains (see page 51).

Places to Visit

Gáldar
Museum, Town Hall

Casa-Museo de Antonio Padrón
1 Calle Drago, Moya

Casa Museo Tomás Morales
1 Paseo Tomás Morales
Open: Monday-Friday 3-5pm,
Saturday and Sunday 10am-2pm.

Tafira
Jardín Canario
Open: daily, but closes 1-3pm.
Admission free.

Teror
Casa-Museo Patronas de la Virgen
Open: daily apart from Fridays and when the family is in residence in the summer.

San Mateo
Casa-Museo de Chó Zacarías
Avenida Tinamar

ACCOMMODATION

Most holidaymakers will arrive in Gran Canaria with accommodation already booked as part of an inclusive package. Hotels in Gran Canaria are graded from one to five stars, *hostals* from one to three stars, and *pensiones* from one to two stars. Accommodation is grouped as follows: H – Hotel, HR – Residential Hotel (no dining room), HA – Hotel Apartments (or Apartotel), RA – Serviced Apartments (no dining room), P – *Pensiones*, little different from *hostals*, CV – Vacation Complex (hotel with sports facilities). Apartments are also graded – from one to three keys.

In summer, both the sea and swimming pools are pleasantly warm, but only masochists will find either to their liking at other times. Most hotels heat their pools, but only to 25°C (77°F), around 3°C below comfort level. To find pleasantly warm water in winter it is necessary to visit public pool complexes.

Those who have not already reserved accommodation will find that the tourist offices at Gando airport, Playa del Inglés or Las Palmas will be able to assist. Spanish National Tourist Offices can supply, on application before departure, lists of accommodation in Gran Canaria, including current tariffs.

ARRIVAL

Virtually all holidaymakers now fly to Gran Canaria, arriving at Gando Airport. There are bargain-priced chartered flights and packages available for last minute bookings, particularly before and after the Christmas and Easter holiday periods. Baggage and immigration clearances are usually speedy, particularly for visitors from EU countries. Tour operators transport those who have booked accommodation with them to their hotels or apartments by coach.

Gando airport is approximately a 30-minute drive away from Las Palmas and 40 minutes from the southern resorts.

Visitors travelling independently will find that the half-hourly bus 60 to Las Palmas operates 24 hours a day from directly outside the airport concourse. In the other direction, the hourly bus 66 runs to Playa del Inglés between 7.15am and 10.15pm.

Gando airport is 22km (13½ miles) from Las Palmas and 30km (18½ miles) from Playa del Inglés; the telephone number is ℡ 928 254140.

BANKS & MONEY

Most banks are open Monday to Friday 9.30am-2pm (1pm Saturday). Specialist exchange organisations operate for most of the day and claim 'no commission', however, their rates will be disadvantageous and they should be avoided where possible. Passports must always be presented when changing traveller's cheques or using cards for obtaining cash. The questions asked vary according to the bank, but many still wish to know your address in Spain; if this is uncertain, just give the name of your last or any local hotel – no-one cares in any case. Eurocheques have the

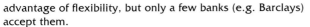

advantage of flexibility, but only a few banks (e.g. Barclays) accept them.

Most hotels, shops and restaurants accept traveller's cheques without charges, but few give a favourable rate, so they are better changed at a bank.

Major credit cards are widely accepted in the main resorts, and as the conversion by credit card companies is usually at a good rate, this is often the best method of payment.

BEACHES & WATERSPORTS

Much of Gran Canaria's coastline is indented with beaches of some sort; many are of dark-grey volcanic sand, but natural golden sands are found at Las Palmas, Playa del Inglés and Maspalomas. Puerto Rico and neighbouring developments, such as Anfi Beach, and Playa de los Amadores, on the south-west coast, also have pale sand, imported from elsewhere.

Due to currents and rock formations, some beaches are dangerous for swimmers; where this is the case, it is indicated in the text.

Strong winds blow almost perpetually on the south-east beaches, making them ideal for surfers and windsurfers. Sub-aqua enthusiasts are recommended to head for the more sheltered bays of the south-west coast, in particular that of Pasito Blanco.

CHEMISTS

In Spain, chemists supply only pharmaceutical products, not toiletries or perfumes. A green cross and the word Farmacia signifies a chemists shop. Most close Saturday afternoons, Sundays and public holidays, but the name and address of the nearest chemist open will always be displayed. Antibiotics can be obtained legally without a prescription. Viagra can also be obtained without a prescription at most chemists, but they are break-ing the law. Press reports indicate that Viagra is significantly cheaper in the Canaries than elsewhere: this is untrue.

CLIMATE

Gran Canaria's weather is discussed in the Introduction, where the average temperatures and rainfall are indicated in the charts. Remember that cloud is affected by the mountains and wind direction, so that it may be cloudy or raining in the northern half of the island while the south basks in glorious sunshine – when the wind, on rare occasions, switches to the south-west the reverse situation can prevail.

CLOTHING

Gran Canaria is never really cold at sea level but early mornings and evenings in winter can be cool enough to require a jacket or pullover to be worn. In the mountains, temperatures fall dramatically as the sun begins to sink or is obscured by cloud, and those planning a lengthy hike among them at any time of the year should take warm clothing – just in case. Nevertheless, unlike the islands of Tenerife and La Palma, snow occurs only rarely on the mountain-tops of Gran Canaria.

Most visitors will find that clothing in Gran Canaria is not particularly cheap, and are advised to bring sufficient with them. Only rarely will anything more that a tee-shirt or blouse, together with shorts or slacks – plus a bikini for the beach – be needed during the day in the sunny south, so do not overpack. Men intending to dine in smart hotels or attend a casino should bring a jacket and tie. Formal dress is never obligatory.

DUTY FREE ALLOWANCES

Although part of Spain the Canaries remain outside the European Customs Union (due to a special arrangement) and therefore duty is applied to visitors on their return to EU countries as though they had been to a non-EU country. Allowances for the UK are: one litre of spirits plus two litres of table wines, or two litres of fortified wines; 200 cigarettes or 100 cigarillos or 50 cigars or 250gms of tobacco; 60ml of perfume or 250ml of toilet water. Other items up to £145 in value are also admitted duty free, but if a single item exceeds that amount, the duty on its full value must be paid. It is not permitted for a group of people to pool their allowances in order to purchase a duty-free item that exceeds £145 in value and take it back without paying the full duty.

ELECTRICITY

Most electricity supply in Gran Canaria is 220-225AC; only in out-of-the-way villages or very old premises will 110-125AC be encountered. The usual continental two-point plugs are accepted, but they are just too small for the British equivalent and an adapter, which can be purchased in the UK, will be needed.

FESTIVALS & SPECIAL EVENTS

The dates of some festivals are based on the variable Christian calendar and will change slightly each year. The exact dates may be found either from the Spanish National Tourist Office in advance, or on arrival in Gran Canaria. Some of the fiestas are described in the text. The venues indicated here are where the most important celebrations take place, but other festivals are also held on the island.

6 January
Las Palmas, Teror, Agüimes, Gáldar: **Cabalgata de los Rey Magos** (The three Kings Horseback Parade)

20 January
Tejeda and Valsequillo: **Almond Blossom festival**

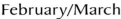

February/March

Las Palmas: Opera Festival
Santa Catalina quarter of Las Palmas, Telde, Agüimes, San Agustín, Maspalomas and Playa del Inglés: **Carnaval**. Carnaval in the southern resorts follows that of Las Palmas

March/April

All the island:
Semana Santa (Holy Week)

29 April

Fortaleza de Ansite, Las Palmas:
Anniversary of Gran Canaria's incorporation into the Crown of Castile

May

Gáldar, Teror, San Nicolás: **Fiesta de San Isidro**

May/June

Las Palmas, Arucas: **Corpus Christi**

29 June

Las Palmas: **Foundation of Las Palmas**

6 July

Fataga: **Fiesta del Albaricoque** (apricots)

25 July

Gáldar, San Bartolomé de Tirajana: **Feast Day of St James** (Santiago), who is the Patron Saint of Spain

4 August

Puerto de las Nieves and Agaete: **Bajada de la Rama**

8 September

Teror: **Romería de la Virgen del Pino**

10 September

Puerto de la Aldea: **Fiesta del Charco**

October (first Sunday)

Puerto de la Luz, Las Palmas: **Fiesta de la Naval** (celebrates the defeat of Sir Francis Drake's fleet in 1595 and may not, therefore, be of great appeal to chauvinistic British holidaymakers)

October

Agüimes: **Fiesta de la Traide del Gofio y Agua** (Festival of the Bringing of Maize and Water)

November

Teror: **Fiesta del Rancho de Animas**

December (first fortnight)

Santa Lucía, Arucas, Gáldar: **Fiesta de la Luz** (Festival of light)

31 December

Las Canteras Beach, Las Palmas: **New Year's Eve celebrations**

FOOD & DRINK

Food and drink in Gran Canaria is described generally in the Introduction. Canarian specialities are rather limited, but visitors may wish to seek out the following:

Baifo	kid braised in a piquant sauce	*Cazuela*	fish stew with potatoes and saffron
Bienmesabes	a sweet confection of honey, eggs and almonds	*Cebolla boba*	pickled onion

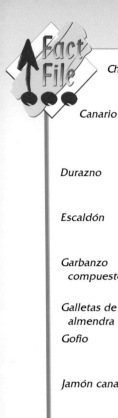

Fact File

Cheme	a local coarse-textured fish, frequently salted
Canario	thick soup made with local vegetables (also known as *puchero*)
Durazno	peach (*melo-cotón* also, as on the mainland)
Escaldón	juice from a *cazuela* fish stew with *gofio* added
Garbanzo compuesto	chick-pea and potato stew with *gofio*
Galletas de almendra	almond biscuits
Gofio	toasted flour, traditionally ground maize
Jamón canario	leg of roast pork, served cold with hot *papas arrugadas* and *mojo picón*. More commonly, and correctly, known as *Pata de Cerdo*
Matalahuva	cumin-flavoured bread
Miel de palma	honey made from the sap of the palm tree – a speciality of the island of La Palma
Mojo	sauces, usually served cold, made with a base of oil, vinegar, garlic and salt. *Mojo picón*, a fiery red version, which incorporates pimentos, is the most popular. *Mojo verde*'s green colour
	comes from the addition of fresh coriander leaves. Both may be obtained, bottled, in supermarkets
Papas arrugadas	very small Canary potatoes, boiled in salt water and served in their jackets: hence, *arrugadas* (wrinkled); usually accompanied by *mojo picón*.
Papas turradas	Canary potatoes roasted or grilled
Papas viudas	roast potatoes with ham and vegetables
Pera-melón	pear-melon, a locally grown fruit
Plátanos Canarias	bananas cooked in brandy
Potaje de berros	watercress soup
Puchero	a thick stew, (also *cocido*)
Quesadilla	cheesecake from the island of Hierro
Queso de flor	goat's milk cheese flavoured with flowers from the cardoom thistle: made in Guía
Rancho Canario	thick vegetable soup with *gofio* and sometimes pork
Rapaduras	confection of honey and almonds from La Palma island
Ropa vieja	literally 'old clothes', a dish of left-overs, mainly found in *tapas* bars

Sancocho	fish, usually salted cherne, poached with potatoes. *Mojo picón* and dried fruit or a sweet fudge based on *gofio* is served with the dish. *Sancocho* is popular for Sunday lunch		which are available in the Christmas period, made in the shape of small fish, hence the name, meaning 'Christmas trout'.	
Truchas navideñas	pastries filled with almonds, yams and pumpkin,	*Turrón*	chewy confection of honey and *gofio*	
		Viejas	local fish with a course texture, always expensive	

HEALTH

As Gran Canaria is a member of the European Union, free health facilities are available to visitors from other countries within the union – an E111 form must be obtained from a Post Office before departure. However, private health insurance is still advisable to ensure prompt attention. No particular health problems are posed in Gran Canaria, apart from the possibility of 'Spanish tummy' for those not used to continental food, or an excess of alcohol. Should problems persist, the local chemist will be able to supply a specific remedy, including antibiotics if necessary.

LANGUAGE

Castillian Spanish is spoken throughout the island but, unlike peninsular Spaniards, Canarios never lisp the letters c or z, and they often omit to pronounce the letter s. The lilting manner of speaking is reminiscent of South American countries, and so are some of the words used, e.g. *guagua* for bus, rather than *autobus* and *papas* for potatoes, rather than *patates*. An accent above a vowel indicates where the stress should be placed; a wiggly line above an 'n' (ñ) means a 'ny' sound rather than an 'n' sound, e.g. the country's name (España) is pronounced 'Espanya', not 'A spanner'.

Many Canarios, particularly those working in the tourist industry, now speak English.

MAPS

The maps printed in this book highlight the location of places of visitor interest, but a large scale road map is recommended for motoring. A good scale map of the island is issued by the tourist board free of charge, however some destinations are not pinpointed accurately enough. Firestone also publish a map of the island, which is somewhat clearer,

albeit to a smaller scale. A map published by Manuel Brito
Auyanet is quite easy to follow and widely available on the
island.

Most published street plans of Las Palmas, due to the shape of the
city, are orientated east/west, rather than the usual north/south, which
can be confusing.

MEASUREMENTS

As may be expected, the metric system is used exclusively. When
shopping, it is helpful to remember that 100 grams is slightly less that
¼ lb and 1 kilogram is slightly more than 2lb. A kilometre measures
between ½ and ¾ of a mile; there are almost precisely 8km to 5 miles.

MOTORING

Many will wish to hire a car for at least part of the holiday. A national
driving licence for any EU country is valid throughout Spain, but UK
visitors must also produce their passports for identification. Virtually all
hire companies accept major credit cards, which are the simplest method
of payment, and avoid the otherwise obligatory deposit that is required.
Local tax is added to the final bill. Due to the small size of the island,
most hire companies do not charge a distance supplement – but check.
Also check if driving on unsurfaced roads is forbidden by the hire company.

The holidaymaker's travel insurance may already cover against accident
– if not, take comprehensive insurance. The names of every person that
may possibly drive the car should be included on the agreement. Ensure
that all the vehicles controls are understood and in working order before
driving away, and obtain a 24-hour contact telephone number.

Do not leave anything in parked cars (see Security).

Most service stations are closed on Sundays.

Main roads in Gran Canaria are given a C prefix, except the *autopista*,
which is called GC1, and minor roads that are surfaced are also numbered,
eg 6.1. Unfortunately for motorists who are not familiar with the island,
road numbers, all too frequently, are not indicated.

Rules of the road
- Drive on the right
- Give precedence to other drivers approaching from the right at
  junctions or roundabouts
- Vehicles must never be parked on a single line, nor must they face
  oncoming traffic
- Speed limits are currently: built-up zones 40km/hr, dual carriageways
  (*carreteras*) 90km/hr, and the motorway (*autopista*) 120km/hr, and
  these must be strictly observed in order to avoid confrontation with the
  traffic police (Guardia Civil)
- Parking facilities are indicated by 'Aparcamiento', no parking by
  'Estacionamiento Prohibido'

- 'Cedo el Paso' means give right of way.
- The Canarios do not, in general, drive as aggressively as their mainland counterparts. Unless in an hurry, let locals pass wherever it is safe to do so.

MUSEUMS

There are few museums in Gran Canaria, and most are concentrated in the Vegueta quarter of Las Palmas. Rarely is an entry charge made, with the notable exception of the Museo de Arte Sacro, which has to be entered in order to tour the interior of the cathedral.

POSTAGE

Most who have spent a holiday in Gran Canaria will return home long before their postcard to the next-door-neighbour has arrived. To speed things up, bring pre-typed, addressed brown envelopes which will take the usual postcard size, and insert the card thereby fooling the 'system', which judges tourist postcards to be extremely non-urgent mail. When purchasing a card also buy a stamp at the same venue, or at a tobacconists as a last resort. Never go to a Post Office (*Correo*) just for stamps – the queues can be horrendous.

PUBLIC HOLIDAYS

1 January	**New Year's Day**
6 January	**Epiphany**
February/March	**Shrove Tuesday** (Las Palmas)
19 March	**Feast of San José** (St Joseph)
March/April	**Maundy Thursday**
	Good Friday
1 May	**Labour Day**
May	**Corpus Christi Day**
	Ascension Day
29 June	**Feast Day of San Pedro and San Pablo**
18 July	**National Day**
25 July	**Feast Day of St James** (Santiago)
15 August	**Assumption Day**
12 October	**Día de la Hispanidad** (Discovery of America Day)
1 November	**All Saints Day**
6 December	**National Constitution Day**
8 December	**Feast Day of the Immaculate Conception of Mary**
25 December	**Christmas Day**

RADIO

Local broadcasts in English are particularly useful for weather forecasts and special events in Gran Canaria. Check the wavebands and programme times on arrival. The BBC World Service can also be heard on short-wave, and occasionally, at night, BBC Radio 4 can be received, particularly in Las Palmas.

SECURITY

Visitors should be security conscious at all times. While crime is not a major problem, tourists – in particular those with hire cars – are the targets for petty theft. While the greatest risk is in the capital and the large resorts, small towns are not immune. Try to park where illegal activity will be more easily noticed, and do not leave *anything* in the car, even in the boot. If possible, remove the hire company's name stickers, which advertise the fact that the car is being used by a tourist.

In Las Palmas, particular care should be taken along Pasco de las Canteras late at night; muggers are not unknown!

SHOPPING

In spite of the island's duty-free status, and low taxes, bargains are now rare. If a purchase is made it is essential to obtain an internationally-valid guarantee, and to buy only from a reputable shop; it is also important to know in advance the lowest price that is being asked for the same item in duty-free shops at departure airports, and even, in some cases, in the high street at home. Bear in mind the £145 limit permitted by Customs and Excise to returning EU visitors.

Alcoholic drinks in litre bottles and cigarettes (by the carton) are best purchased in large *supermercados* (supermarkets), the further away from tourist areas the better. Canary souvenirs of quality include embroidery (but watch out for fake imports), palm-leaf baskets and knives and boxes made of bone with inlay metalwork. Cigar lovers should try Palmitos cigars, which come from the island of La Palma, and Miel de Palma palm tree honey, from the same island. Shops open generally 9am-1pm and 4-7pm, although the large department stores forego the afternoon siesta.

TELEPHONES

A 928 prefix must be dialled, even within Gran Canaria, for all local calls. Many public kiosks, usually painted yellow and displaying the word *Teléfono*, may be used for international calls. Remember to check if there is a time difference involved. To make a call from Gran Canaria to any-where in the United Kingdom, dial 0044, pause for the tone, followed by the local code, omitting the initial 0, and then the number.

To make a call to Gran Canaria from Europe dial 0034 928 followed by the number.

TIME

At the time of writing, unlike mainland Spain, but like the United Kingdom, The Canary Islands follow Greenwich Mean Time in winter, and are one hour ahead of it in summer.

TIPPING

A service charge is included in most bills, and no additional gratuity is expected: this includes all hotel and restaurant bills and taxi fares. However, for good personal service a small tip is appreciated.

TOILET FACILITIES

Public toilets are virtually non-existent in Gran Canaria, apart from the airport and the Estación de Guaguas in Las Palmas. However, no bars, restaurants or hotels may, by law, refuse the use of their facilities to anyone, including non-customers.

General terms denoting toilets are: *servicios*, *lavabos* and *aseos*; *señores* or *caballeros* denote men's toilets, and *señoras* or *señyoretes* women's toilets. Signs rather than words are used on occasions – do not confuse the woman making up her lips with the man smoking his pipe – both are quite similar!

TOURIST INFORMATION OFFICES

Spanish Tourist Board Office in UK
22-23 Manchester Square, London W1M 5AP, ☎ 0207 486 8077/85/33, Fax: 0207 486 8034, Web site www.tourspain.es

Tourist Information Offices in Gran Canaria are listed at the end of each chapter.

TRANSPORT (PUBLIC)

Buses

Not all holidaymakers to Gran Canaria opt to hire a car for all, or even part of their stay, but many will wish to explore the island without having to resort to coach excursions. They are well catered for by the local bus services, which link almost every part of Gran Canaria, no matter how remote.

Throughout this book the numbers of the buses that follow the itineraries described have been given and no changes are planned following the recent merger of the island's two bus companies Salcai and Utinsa, now known as Global. It is recommended that a choice of the itineraries that appeal is made at an early stage, and the numbers of the relevant buses and their timetables checked out locally.

Those staying in the south can obtain travel information from the Tourist Office at the Yumbo Centrum in Playa del Inglés.

Bus stops are indicated by a sign with a blue circle surrounded by a red line, and bearing a red diagonal stripe, the word bus and a large P (for *Parada*) will be displayed. Confusingly, many bus stops in the south bear a Palmitos Park Bus Stop sign; although buses to Palmitos Park do stop at them, so also do buses on other routes.

Many buses terminate in Las Palmas at the subterranean Estación de Guaguas, facing Parque de San Telmo. From here, Tarjete tickets may be purchased, for 2,000 pesetas each, which may be used on all public bus services at an economical rate. Single tickets are sold on the bus but the cost will be higher if several journeys are made. It is necessary to ascend the stairs or ramp from the bus station to Parque de San Telmo for the municipal bus (guagua) stops.

A half price return ticket from Las Palmas to the southern resorts is available on Sundays and public holidays – but not in the reverse direction.

All tickets must be inserted in the cancelling machine on the vehicle, which is entered from the front and vacated from the rear. It will help to follow a map in case the bus driver forgets the destination requested. Most buses have a red button, which should be pushed just before disembarking. At bus stops, raise an arm to halt a bus.

Tartanas

These horse-drawn open carriages, operating only in Las Palmas, can hardly be termed public transport, but they offer a leisurely, if expensive, way of seeing the city. Up to four people can be seated in a *tartana*, and the price charged is for the vehicle, not per person. A regular pick-up point is the Hotel Santa Catalina, in Parque Doramas, and the Parque de Santa Catalina area. Tariffs appear to be negotiable.

Taxis

No duty and low tax once meant cheap taxi fares throughout the Canaries but, sadly, this is no longer the case. It is important, therefore, for most visitors to become acquainted with the buses as soon as possible. In Las Palmas taxi fares are always metered, but in other locations they are sometimes not – negotiate in advance: all taxi drivers must carry a fares chart in their cab. A *libre* sign denotes that the taxi is free; at night, this is supplemented by a green light.

WATER

Tap water, although safe in most tourist areas and Las Palmas, is rarely drunk in Gran Canaria. Mineral water, still (*sin gas*) or sparkling (*con gas*), is readily available and cheaper if purchased in litre bottle size or even larger from supermarkets, although the relatively expensive smaller sizes can be useful for the beach. Firgas, bottled from a spring in Gran Canaria, is the most popular brand throughout the Canary Islands.

· INDEX ·

LANDMARK
VISITORS GUIDES

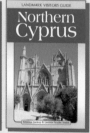

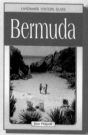

To order send a cheque (check)/Visa/MasterCard details to: Landmark Publishing,
Waterloo House, 12 Compton, Ashbourne, Derbyshire DE6 IDA England
Tel: 01335 347349 Fax: 01335 347303 e-mail: landmark@clara.net
web site: www.landmarkpublishing.co.uk

* In USA order from **Hunter Publishing**
130 Campus Drive, Edison NJ 08818, Tel (732) 225 1900 or (800) 255 0343
Fax: (732) 417 0482 www.hunterpublishing.com

Provence*
ISBN: 1 901522 45 8
240pp,
UK £10.95 US $17.95

Côte d'Azur*
ISBN: 1 901522 29 6
144pp,
UK £6.95 US $13.95

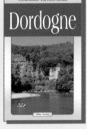

Dordogne
ISBN: 1 901522 67 9
224pp,
UK £11.95

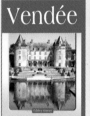

Vendée
ISBN: 1 901522 76 X
96pp,
UK £4.95

Languedoc
ISBN: 1 901522 79 2
144pp,
UK £7.95

Bruges*
ISBN: 1 901522 66 0
96pp,
UK £5.95

Ticino
ISBN: 1 901522 74 1
192pp
UK £8.95

Italian Lakes*
ISBN: 1 901522 11 3
240pp,
UK £11.95 US $15.95

Riga*
ISBN: 1 901522 59 8
160pp,
UK £7.95

Cracow
ISBN: 1 901522 54 7
160pp,
UK £7.95

Iceland*
ISBN: 1 901522 68 7
192pp,
UK £9.95

Sri Lanka
ISBN: 1 901522 37 7
192pp,
UK £9.95

India: Kerala
ISBN: 1 901522 16 4
256pp,
UK £10.99

India: Goa
ISBN: 1 901522 23 7
160pp,
UK £7.95

New Zealand*
ISBN: 1 901522 36 9
320pp
UK £12.95 US $18.95

Prices subject to alteration from time to time

LANDMARK VISITORS

(See page 109 for mailing details)

Cornwall*
ISBN: 1 901522 09 1
256pp, £10.95

Devon
ISBN: 1 901522 42 3
224pp, £9.95

Dorset
ISBN: 1 901522 46 6
240pp, £9.95

Somerset
ISBN: 1 901522 40 7
224pp, £10.95

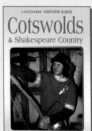

Cotswolds
ISBN: 1 901522 12 1
224pp, £9.99

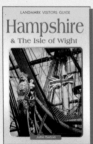

Hampshire
ISBN: 1 901522 14 8
224pp, £9.95

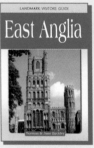

East Anglia
ISBN: 1 901522 58 X
224pp, £9.95

Scotland*
ISBN: 1 901522 18 0
288pp, £11.95

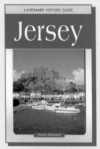

Jersey
ISBN: 1 901522 47 4
224pp, £9.99

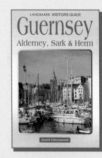

Guernsey
ISBN: 1 901522 48 2
224pp, £9.95

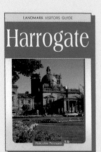

Harrogate
ISBN: 1 901522 55 5
96pp, £4.95

GUIDES TO THE UK

* available in the USA

Lake District*

ISBN: 1 901522 38 5
224pp, £9.95

Peak District

ISBN: 1 901522 25 3
240pp, £9.99

Yorkshire Dales

ISBN: 1 901522 41 5
224pp, £10.95

West Cornwall
ISBN: 1 901522 24 5
96pp, £5.95

South Devon
ISBN: 1 901522 52 0
96pp, £5.95

Southern Peak
ISBN: 1 901522 27 X
96pp, £5.95

Southern Lakeland
ISBN: 1 901522 53 9
96pp, £5.95

Dartmoor
ISBN: 1 901522 69 5
96pp, £5.95

Isle of Wight
ISBN: 1 901522 71 7
112pp, £6.55

Hereford
ISBN: 1 901522 72 5
96pp, £5.95

Prices subject to alteration from time to time

Published by
Landmark Publishing Ltd.
Waterloo House, 12 Compton, Ashbourne, Derbyshire DE6 1DA England
Tel: (01335) 347349 Fax: (01335) 347303 e-mail: landmark@clara.net

ISBN 1 901 522 19 9

© **Christopher Turner 2000**

2nd Edition

The rights of Christopher Turner as author of this work
have been asserted by him in accordance with the Copyright,
Design and Patents Act, 1993.

British Library Cataloguing in Publication Data: a catalogue record for this
book is available from the British Library.

Print: Gutenberg Press Ltd, Malta

Cartography & design: Samantha Witham

Front cover: Anfi Beach, Puerto Rico

Back cover top: Arucus; **bottom:** Playa del Inglés

Picture Credits

All photography supplied by Christopher Turner except:-

Gran Canaria Tourist Board: Back cover top,
8, 22, 42, 44, 52/3, 54, 56, 58, 80, 82, 87, 90

International Photobank: 6, 13, 32, 47, 72, 75, 89